MW00576379

DBT Workbook For Depression

The Complete Guide for Treating Depression & Anxiety with Dialectical Behavior Therapy | DBT Skills for Men & Women for Mindfulness, Happiness and Emotional Health

By Barrett Huang

https://barretthuang.com/

FREE Guide: Mastering DBT Essentials

FREE DOWNLOAD ALERT!

Master Dialectical Behavior Therapy Skills in 5 Simple Steps with my Free DBT Quick Guide. Access the 'Mastering DBT Essentials' quick guide at:

https://barretthuang.com/dbt-quick-guide/

Or scan the code below:

Contents

Introduction

"Depression is the most unpleasant thing I have ever experienced. It is that absence of being able to envisage that you will ever be cheerful again. The absence of hope."
– J.K. Rowling

The school bell rings for lunch. The class erupts into wild noise, and everybody talks all at once. I slowly stand up, hunch over to grab my backpack, and quietly leave the room.

I walk across the halls amidst all the excited chatter and chaos. I don't greet anyone, and no one greets me. I reach the cafeteria, but I don't go in for lunch. I walk on until I reach the library. Once inside, I go to my favorite dark corner, and as quietly as possible, I bring out my lunch and eat silently.

Since there are no distractions, I finish lunch in record time. However, my next class is still far off, so I fall asleep in my little dark corner. (I'm so tired and sleepy all the time.)

I get back to class, and the afternoon just goes on and on and on. The bell rings, and nearly everyone jumps out of their seats. Kids are grabbing bags, heading out the door, and making plans with each other. Just like that, the room is empty.

I grab my bag, go out the door, and slowly walk home. Once I reach home, I head straight to my room and close the door. I don't let anyone know I'm back, and no one notices me. My day is almost done. And just like yesterday, I feel invisible.

The above is how I spent most of my teenage years— in complete loneliness and isolation. Even now, I find it difficult to remember and put into words this very difficult time in my life.

As I started my journey to mental healing, I discovered everything that caused my mental health problems. Let me start at the beginning...

My Story

My parents emigrated from China to Canada in the 1980s. My sister and I were born in Toronto. English is our first language, so there was no "language barrier" to overcome. We also attended a multicultural school, so our cultural identity, at least on the surface, was not an issue. It was everything else that was the problem.

Although the intention was to provide a better future for the family, I always resented why my parents were so stuck in their old-fashioned Chinese ways. This created a chaotic situation for me because, at home, everything was Chinese, but outside, everything was Canadian. It felt like being in two different worlds but not belonging in either.

My father was a hoarder who suffered from undiagnosed Obsessive-Compulsive Disorder (OCD). One of his compulsions was to have everything he had arranged a certain way and located in a specific place. He would get upset if something wasn't where it was supposed to be. Imagine living in a house where you were afraid to touch anything and couldn't return things where they belonged. Also, since he was a hoarder, our home was always cluttered.

My mother had undiagnosed General Anxiety Disorder (GAD). She was constantly worried about something and always expected some disaster to strike at any moment. For example, despite living in a safe and secure neighborhood, she constantly worried that someone would enter our house. Imagine living in a home where you were continuously alerted that something terrible would happen at any time.

She also had a victim mindset. I heard the phrase, *"Why is this happening to me?"* way too often at home. She saw herself as the victim of circumstances, other people, or the world. She hardly ever saw her part or responsibility in situations.

Please note that I'm not sharing these stories about my parents because I blame them. In truth, I have a lot of empathy for them. And when I look back at my childhood, there was love too, and I know in my heart that they were doing their best.

Still, this does not change the reality that I grew up in a very chaotic and unstable home with parents suffering from mental health disorders. Our Chinese culture also meant that we were not in the habit of talking about our feelings. (It's seen as a sign of weakness.) Physical displays of affection were also nonexistent. These left my sister and me feeling emotionally unstable growing up.

By the time I hit my teenage years, I was already showing symptoms of OCD and GAD. (I would later be diagnosed with these disorders by a mental health professional.)

One of my compulsions was a morning ritual I had to go through before school. Do you remember the British pop girl band, the *Spice Girls*? When I was 14, I had a huge crush on Emma Bunton. One morning ritual was standing in front of her poster, talking to myself, and pretending I was courting or dating her. (Never mind that she was much older than me.) I would talk and fantasize until I felt "just right."

This particular compulsion of mine could take 10 minutes or go on for hours. As it's a compulsion, I MUST do it. I won't want to attend school if I don't reach that "just right" feeling.

Sometimes, I would skip sleep altogether to avoid this morning ritual because I knew I would have to go through the whole routine again the next day. As you can imagine, my sleeping schedule was a mess, and I would be tired and sleepy all day at school.

Another compulsion I had was not stepping on lines or cracks in the pavement. If I did, my anxiety would kick in, and I would be nervous the whole day as I waited for something bad to happen.

As a person with anxiety, that persistent sense of dread is hardwired into my psyche. Even today, I still fear that the house will burn down if I don't double-check the stove, and I sometimes check the tap 2-3 times to ensure it's completely turned off. When I leave, I sometimes triple-check that the door is locked because my mind tells me someone will break in and steal everything. (Yes, just like my mom.)

OCD and GAD disorders are very draining. And they contributed heavily to my depression.

The teenage years are supposed to be a time of change, new experiences, going out with friends, and excitement about the future. I had none of that. In fact, I didn't have any friends in a school of about 5,000 kids, so I was incredibly lonely. This loneliness made me self-isolate, and this made me sink deeper and deeper into pain and despair.

I started this section with a quote by J.K. Rowling because that's exactly how I felt for the longest time. For years, I couldn't see myself ever being cheerful again, and I had no hope for the future.

Fortunately, things started to change when I left home for college at 19. I was in a new environment and welcomed returning to my dorm room each day. Even though I was still very much alone, at least the space I came back to was not as chaotic and unstable as my home life.

In my 20s, I realized what I experienced as a child was abnormal. I needed to get away from the situation to improve my life and mindset—so I started to travel. Ironically, my first stop was China.

I was curious about the history of my parents and wanted to see where they came from. While there, I discovered the hardships my parents went through growing up. It made me realize how lucky I am to grow up in a free country. I also learned that my parents went through the Great Chinese Famine, where 30-40 million people starved to death in China, and experienced the Cultural Revolution, where another 10 million died. My parents never even had the chance to go to college. All of this helped me understand why my parents are the way they are.

It's strange to be at odds with my parents when I was constantly around them— and then to understand them once I was gone and visited where they came from. For the first time, I could see things from their perspective and developed a lot of empathy for them.

From China, I traveled to other Asian countries such as South Korea, Hong Kong, Thailand, and the Philippines. I actually stayed in South Korea for three years, teaching English as a Second Language (ESL). To this day, I consider it as one of the best decisions I've ever made. It made me independent and teaching gave me a sense of fulfillment I've never felt before.

Traveling opened my mind to different cultures and different ways of life. It also showed me how other people faced adversity. Some of the places I visited were impoverished. Yet, the people I met were so courageous and nearly everyone had a smile. They gave me hope, and I began believing I could overcome my mental hardships. I started to see some light at the end of the tunnel.

I came back to Toronto after about four years. As I figured out what to do next with my life, I also started educating myself about my mental health problems. I read many self-help books and reached the point where I felt ready and open to treatment. I met a psychologist and was officially diagnosed with OCD and GAD.

I was prescribed anti-anxiety medication and underwent psychotherapy, specifically Cognitive Behavior Therapy (CBT). After a while, I had improved to the point where I asked my doctor to lower my dosage. (For the record, I still take anti-anxiety medication, which helps me keep this disorder under control.) At some point, I noticed that CBT was no longer working for me, so I began exploring other psychotherapy treatments.

I discovered Dialectical Behavior Therapy (DBT), the treatment that I credit for enabling me to finally break free from the mental health issues preventing me from living the life I wanted.

I still experience OCD, GAD, and depression from time to time. I don't believe they will ever entirely disappear, but they no longer debilitate me. I've coped and adjusted. I'm calmer and more level-headed now, and I have the courage—and tools—to deal with life's obstacles better than before. And yes, I'll dare say it—I experience happiness now and hope. It's my sincerest wish that you achieve the same with this book.

Who Should Read This Book

This book is for everyone experiencing even the most minor symptoms of depression. You may want to read this book to understand better what you're going through, or you may already be in therapy and wish to include the exercises in this book in your treatment plan.

This book is also for anyone who knows someone struggling with depression. One of the first things we can do to help and support someone we care about is to understand their situation better. Understanding allows you to empathize, which people experiencing depression would highly appreciate.

Goals of This Book

This book seeks to help people get a better understanding of depression and to give them real-life tools to help them cope with this condition.

I was very confused about my mental health disorders. I was miserable and knew things needed to change, but I didn't even have the words to describe what I felt or thought (let alone what caused them!). So, it is my sincere hope that this book gives you clarity. Awareness and understanding are fundamental when dealing with mental health problems.

But, of course, knowing about your condition is just half the battle, and the rest is learning how to cope and, hopefully, heal. This is where the second part of the book comes in.

Dialectical Behavior Therapy (DBT) is the method that truly enabled me to deal effectively with my co-existing mental health disorders. I'll discuss this technique in detail and provide plenty of exercises to help you effectively adopt it in your life.

Content Warning

This book contains topics that may be distressing or disturbing. Some stories, topics, and incidents may prompt or trigger you. Loneliness, sadness, emotional abuse, feelings of worldliness, loss, breakups, self-harm, and death are examples of such content. Please be mindful of these and other issues that may trouble you. Reminder: please don't hesitate to ask for assistance or consult a specialist whenever you feel overwhelmed.

Safety

When dealing with depression, *safety* is essential. As mentioned, topics and stories in this book may trigger you, so it's good to take steps to *be safe* and *feel safe* while reading this book and doing the exercises provided.

How can you feel safe while reading this book? Safety means different things to different people, but the following are some ideas.

- Create a **Safe Space**. Where (or when) do you feel most safe and comfortable? This may be sitting on an old chair from your childhood in your bedroom or alone in the kitchen with a cup of coffee in the mornings. Whatever it is, consider reading this book in that safe space.
- Set a **reading boundary**. Set limits on how much you read and for how long. Take breaks as needed, and remember that it's okay to put the book down if you feel overwhelmed.
- **Self-care checklist**. Take care of your physical and emotional needs while reading. This may involve getting adequate sleep, eating healthily, and participating in activities that make you happy.

- Establish a "**Plan B**." Create a list of actions to take if you ever feel unsafe. Here are a few suggestions:
    - Stop reading.
    - Call _____.
    - Message _____.
    - Go to _____.
    - Listen to _____.
    - Watch _____.
    - Others:

    _____

    _____

    _____

Be Kind to Yourself

Whenever I look back at my adolescent years, I feel a lot of empathy. I struggled so much and went through many years of anxiety and loneliness. I anguished about so many things over which I had no control, and I had no idea how to deal with the things over which I did have influence. This resulted in a lot of anger directed towards myself, others, and life. Of course, this did not help my situation because it only worsened my mental health problems. So, I advise you to be patient, compassionate, and understanding of yourself. Kindness, I firmly believe, is the first step toward healing.

Depression 101

Depression, or major depressive disorder (MDD), is a mood disorder that affects how you feel, think, and act. It's distinguished by persistent feelings of sadness, despair and loss of interest in activities one previously enjoyed. Sadly, depression is a prevalent mental disorder.

According to the World Health Organization (WHO), depression affects around 280 million people globally.[1] In the United States, an estimated 21 million adults (8.4% of the adult population) have experienced at least one major depressive episode in 2020.[2]

Depression may be "common," but there's a lot of confusion and misconceptions about this mental disorder. As I started to understand my depression disorder, I was surprised at how different factors caused and affected each other. For example, the extreme loneliness I felt in my teens contributed to the development of my depression. Then my depression made me want to withdraw even more from social interactions.

My goal with the following sections is to help you develop a deeper understanding of this illness so that you can make the most informed treatment decision possible.

Also, in my experience, understanding my depression made me more open to the help and treatments that were available to me. I hope this also applies to you.

Depression vs. Sadness

Depression and sadness are two distinct emotions. Sadness is a natural human feeling due to an event like a loss or disappointment. It's usually temporary, and people can usually pinpoint the source of their sadness.

Depression, on the other hand, is a mental health condition characterized by a chronic and pervasive sense of melancholy, hopelessness, and loss of interest or pleasure in activities. Depression, unlike sadness, can be unrelated to a specific event and can continue for weeks, months, or even years.

SADNESS	DEPRESSION
A typical human emotion	A mental health disorder
Typically happens in response to an unpleasant event	Happens as a result of genetics, life events, medication, and others
Enables people to function and do daily activities normally	Interferes with daily activities, relationships, and work
Temporary	Constant
Usually goes away with time	Requires intervention such as learning and adopting coping techniques, making lifestyle changes, seeking therapy or medication, etc.

Feelings of sadness are okay. After all, life is full of ups and downs. However, when you don't understand why you're sad, and if you feel this way for long periods that it affects your daily life, it might be depression.

What Causes Depression?

A singular motive does not cause depression; the reasons are complex and can differ for each person. Some of the possible causes of depression include:

1. **Genetics**. Although no specific gene has been linked to depression, studies have indicated that having a close family member with the condition increases your odds of developing it yourself.[3,4]

   Over the years, I've learned that my dad's mother and older brother committed suicide. Looking back at my dad, I don't remember many moments when he was truly happy. So, in my situation, I'm inclined to see my depression and other mental health problems as associated with my genetics.

2. **Brain chemistry**. Changes in the balance of chemicals in the brain, such as *serotonin, norepinephrine*, and *dopamine,* can contribute to depression. Why? One theory suggests that neurotransmitter imbalance may disrupt the communication between brain cells, leading to mood disturbances. Another theory suggests that this imbalance may lead to changes in the structure and function of brain regions involved in regulating mood.

   Serotonin is essential for mood, hunger, and sleep regulation. It's also known as the "happy" hormone. *Norepinephrine* is implicated in the "fight or flight" response of the body. It aids in the regulation of mood, attention, and arousal. Dopamine is involved in the regulation of pleasure and reward. That's why it's also known as the "feel-good" hormone.

3. **Life events**. Trauma, stress, abuse, neglect, loneliness, or significant life changes, such as a death or divorce, can trigger depression.

One of my earliest trauma memories was when I was 11 or 12. My parents were going through a difficult divorce, and my sister and I were caught in the crossfire. There was a lot of fighting, accusations, and ill feelings.

One day, my dad left for work, and my mom suddenly barged into my room, woke me up, and told me to pack a bag quickly because we were going on a trip with her. I refused to go and started crying and screaming.

For some reason, my dad returned, saw what was happening, and whisked me away to stay at a neighbor's house while they talked things out. I returned home, but I remember continuously looking over my shoulder for days. I was scared that my mother was waiting for me around the corner, ready to take me away forever.

4. **Medical conditions**. Chronic illnesses, such as cancer or heart disease, can cause depression.

5. **Substance abuse**. Alcohol and drug abuse can cause depression or worsen existing depression.

6. **Hormonal changes**. Hormonal changes during puberty, pregnancy, or menopause affect mood and may contribute to depression. For this reason, data shows that women are twice to three times more likely to experience depression than men.[5] (Please also see Depression in Women, page 40.)

7. **Medications**. Some drugs, such as birth control pills or blood pressure medication, can cause depression as a side effect.

Depression Signs & Symptoms

The symptoms of depression can vary from person to person, but some common symptoms may include the following:

1. **Constant feelings of sadness, emptiness, or hopelessness.** Depression is marked by an overall bleak outlook regarding life. You feel and believe there's nothing you can do to change or improve your situation, so you don't see how things can improve.

2. **Loss of interest or pleasure in formerly enjoyable activities.** Old hobbies and activities that used to make you happy no longer do, so you avoid them altogether.

3. **Fluctuations in appetite or weight (loss or gain).** You don't care about what you eat or drink, which may result in sudden weight loss or gain.

4. **Sleeping problems.** You might have trouble falling asleep (insomnia) or always sleep too much (hypersomnia).

5. **Loss of energy**. You often feel tired, exhausted, or utterly devoid of energy. You find even the simplest activities (e.g., getting out of bed, brushing your teeth, interacting with others, etc.) exhausting.

6. **Feelings of guilt, self-hate or self-loathing**. You might have low self-esteem and often experience feelings of worthlessness. You may also often judge and criticize yourself. You might also often experience feelings of guilt or always feel that you're "wrong."

7. **Psychomotor agitation or retardation**. You feel restless and exhibit slowed speaking or body movements. You may also have difficulties concentrating, making decisions, or remembering things.

8. **Difficulty handling emotions such as anger or irritability.** Your tolerance level for stressful situations and intense emotions is low, and you may find yourself impulsively reacting to everything and everyone.

9. **Isolation**. You don't feel connected to anyone, so you disengage from family, friends, or life and spend more time alone.

   Important: Isolation can be both a symptom of depression and a cause; for me, it was the latter. The severe loneliness I felt during my teen years led me to self-isolate, and this, in turn, caused my depression.

10. **Thoughts of self-harm, self-mutilation, or suicide ideation**. The hopelessness and deep despair that one feels when depressed may be so severe that thoughts of "ending the suffering" or "escaping the pain" takes over. (It's estimated that up to 60% of people who take their own lives suffer from major depression.[6])

Depression may also manifest in sudden physical changes or problems. This, too, can vary from person to person, but some common physical symptoms may include the following:

1. Headaches and body aches
2. Muscle tension or cramps
3. Digestive problems (e.g., stomach pain, diarrhea, constipation, etc.)
4. Skin problems (e.g., severe acne, eczema, psoriasis, etc.)

Am I suffering from depression? According to the Diagnostic and Statistical Manual of Mental Disorders (DSM-5)[7], a person must experience the following to be diagnosed with clinical depression.

1. A person must have had at least one major depressive episode that lasted at least two weeks.
2. The depressive episode must show at least five of the symptoms mentioned above.

If you haven't been diagnosed yet but are experiencing symptoms of depression, you might want to take the **Depression Self-Assessment** *exercise on page 158.*

Content Warning: the following contains distressing material.

As for me, I experienced all of the above depressive symptoms. Not all of them all the time, but I would suffer for weeks and sometimes months on end. The primary depressive symptom, *feelings of hopelessness*, is something I struggled with for years.

The issue about depression is that it's so many things at once, and each symptom impacts the other that you can quickly become trapped in a vicious spiral. For example, the loneliness and alienation I felt as an adolescent caused me to self-isolate and withdraw from everyone. I turned to internet games and junk food to escape my reality. I'd play for hours, then have a late meal before falling asleep. Exercise had never been a part of my daily regimen.

Sometimes, due to my OCD, I would skip sleep altogether because I didn't want to do my rigid morning ritual. However, OCD or not, I've always had sleep problems, which contributed to my sleepiness, low energy, and lack of focus at school.

Feelings of guilt also plagued me, and in all honesty, I still often do. In Chinese culture, there is a strong emphasis on *filial piety*, which is the idea that children should always obey their parents. Also, the son is supposed to take the reins and eventually care for the family. As a kid, I always felt I wasn't measuring up or doing enough for my family. As an adult, my sister didn't mince words that I was not "stepping up," and my parents would use a lot of emotional blackmail on me. As a result, I still often feel I'm not a good brother or son.

At the back of all this were constant feelings of sadness and hopelessness. I couldn't envision a "tomorrow" or "future" for years. I didn't have any direction in my daily life, so I didn't have any long-term goals. What's the point? I just wanted to get through each day.

My OCD didn't help either, as I had constant intrusive, unwanted thoughts (obsessions) about harming myself.

When I was living alone, there were times when I would go out on my balcony, which was on the 17th floor, and think about what would happen if I jumped. Would I break some bones? Would I become paralyzed? Would I die instantly? But then… at least it would end all of my sufferings. How would my family react if I died? Would they even care? Maybe my sister and parents would stop blaming me for everything.

This constant flow of obsessive thoughts is typical in people with OCD, and it doesn't mean we will take action. However, such thoughts drove me deeper into depression.

What are the Different Types of Depression?

There are various varieties of depression, each with its own set of symptoms and characteristics. These are a few examples of the most prevalent types:

1. **Major Depressive Disorder (MDD)** is the most prevalent type of depression. It involves persistent feelings of sadness, hopelessness, and loss of interest or pleasure in activities.

2. **Persistent Depressive Disorder (PDD)**, also known as *dysthymia*, involves symptoms of depression that persist for at least two years. Although people with PDD experience the same symptoms as MDD, they are usually less severe. Nevertheless, PDD is devastating because symptoms last for an extended period.

3. **Postpartum Depression (PPD)** is a type of depression that can affect new mothers after giving birth. It's different from the "baby blues," a common condition that causes mild mood changes and usually goes away on its own within a week or two after delivery. PPD, on the other hand, can cause severe and long-lasting depression symptoms. (Please also see Depression in Women, page 40.)

4. **Seasonal Affective Disorder (SAD)** is a type of depression related to seasonal changes. It typically occurs in the fall and winter when there is less sunlight and shorter days.

My friend, Ingrid*, lives in Europe, and she said, *"My first recollection of my depression was in my teens, probably around 17. I remember because we have a tradition of having a special dinner to mark the start of fall. It was one of my favorite things, and we would have "family meetings" about the menu. That year though, I didn't have any enthusiasm for it at all.*

As soon as the temperatures started dropping and the sky got darker, I felt miserable. At first, I thought I was just tired, but then the fatigue wouldn't let up. I started to stay longer and longer in bed, and when I finally gathered the strength to get up, it would get dark so soon that I'd feel even gloomier than before.

Winter came and went, and by the time spring rolled over, I was pretty much my old self again that I dismissed it. However, when the season changed to fall, I felt gloomy again. This time, my family was not so understanding.

My parents and siblings thought I was seeking attention, which made me sad and mad. I vented my frustrations about food; as a result, I gained a lot of weight over the winter months.

Even though I gained a lot of weight, I was, again, pretty much like my old self come spring, and I lost all the weight I gained as I became physically active again. Unfortunately, this made my family think I was going through a phase. They almost had me convinced... until fall came again.

This time, my depression hit me hard, and I could barely get out of bed. One day, my mom saw me on the bedroom floor curled in a fetal position sobbing uncontrollably, and when she asked me what was wrong, I said, "Mom, I don't

---

* Name changed for privacy.

know." My mother said that hearing me say that broke her heart, and she knew something was terribly wrong.

My mom contacted a psychotherapist friend, and I was eventually diagnosed with Seasonal Affective Disorder (SAD). I don't take medication; I combine <u>bright light therapy</u> and <u>DBT</u>. I also determined that stress significantly impacts my SAD, so I go almost entirely offline and refrain from checking the news during winter.

5. **Psychotic Depression** is a type of depression that showcases symptoms of depression and symptoms of psychosis. Psychosis is defined as a loss of contact with reality, which can result in delusions, hallucinations, or both. These symptoms can be severe and make it difficult for a person to function daily.

6. **Bipolar Disorder** is a mood disorder that's considered a type of depression because it involves episodes of depression. However, it's different from other types of depression because it also involves episodes of mania or hypomania.

   Mania is a period of abnormally elevated or irritable mood and increased energy. It's a particular time when a person experiences a sustained period of extreme euphoria, excitement, or irritability that is not typical of their usual behavior. The manic episodes are severe and cause serious problems at work, school, or relationships.

   Hypomania is a milder form of mania. During a hypomanic episode, a person may feel unusually energetic or happy, have racing thoughts or speech, and engage in impulsive or risky behavior. Although still very disruptive, a hypomanic episode doesn't usually result in severe problems at work, school, or relationships.

Depression Recommended Treatments

Depression is one of the most prevalent mental health disorders in the world. It's even called the "common cold" of mental health disorders because of its prevalence.

Because depression is so common and yet significantly impacts a person's quality of life, there has been a lot of research and resources devoted to understanding and treating this disorder. The good news is that this has resulted in various treatments available. The bad news is that some of these treatments may be overused even though they may be ineffective, while others may not receive the attention they deserve.

Following are some of the most frequent treatments for depression. As you learn more about them, please note that **since depression is a complicated disorder with multiple causes, no single treatment works for everyone**.

When I started to see a mental health professional, I was prescribed anti-anxiety medication for my GAD. This helped manage some of my symptoms, but I needed psychotherapy to get better truly. I also found physical activities extremely helpful, so I added a fitness routine to my schedule. So, I guess I'm trying to say to please be open-minded and curious. Mental health problems are multifaceted; naturally, you may require a multifaceted approach to treatment as well.

Medication

Depression has been long believed to be caused by a chemical imbalance in the brain. For this reason, antidepressants are prevalent in the market. The most commonly prescribed medication for depression is selective serotonin reuptake inhibitors or SSRIs. They work by increasing *serotonin* levels in the brain, which can help regulate mood. Examples of SSRIs include fluoxetine (Prozac), sertraline (Zoloft), and escitalopram (Lexapro).

Serotonin and norepinephrine reuptake inhibitors (SNRIs) work similarly to SSRIs but also increase levels of *norepinephrine* in the brain. Examples of SNRIs include venlafaxine (Effexor) and duloxetine (Cymbalta).

Next, we have tricyclic antidepressants (TCAs). These medications were some of the earliest antidepressants developed, and they work by increasing levels of serotonin and norepinephrine in the brain. However, they are less commonly prescribed today due to their side effects (e.g., dry mouth, blurred vision, dizziness, increased heart rate, nausea, etc.). Examples of TCAs include amitriptyline (Elavil) and nortriptyline (Pamelor).

Monoamine oxidase inhibitors (MAOIs) are antidepressants that block the enzyme *monoamine oxidase*, which breaks down serotonin and norepinephrine in the brain. They are also less commonly prescribed today due to their side effects and interactions with certain foods and medications. Examples of MAOIs include phenelzine (Nardil) and tranylcypromine (Parnate).

Note: Antidepressants can take several weeks to work and may cause various side effects. If you're taking or thinking of taking medication, please work closely with a healthcare provider to monitor the medication's effectiveness and manage any side effects.

Nearly 85% of people who suffer from depression believe their condition results from abnormal brain chemistry.[8] However, recent research published in the 2022 issue of *Molecular Psychiatry* suggests this may not be true after all.[9]

This recent discovery suggests that prescribed medications may not be the best course of treatment or should not be the first thing to try for depression.

However, please remember that depression is multifaceted, so you shouldn't discount this option altogether. The best recourse is to speak to a mental health expert about which treatments are best for you.

Very Important: If you're taking antidepressants and wish to stop to explore other treatments, please DO NOT do so without assistance from your doctor or a medical health expert. Stopping antidepressant medication alone can be dangerous, leading to potential side effects and severe health risks.[10]

For example, you may experience withdrawal symptoms, mood changes, a relapse or worsening of your condition, increased feelings of self-harm and suicide, and others. This does not mean you cannot stop taking antidepressants once you've begun. The key is slowly reducing your dosage (a.k.a. tapering) and closely monitoring any changes you may experience. And this is best done under the guidance of a mental health professional.

Brain Stimulation Therapy

Brain stimulation therapy uses electrical impulses or magnetic fields to stimulate specific brain areas. The reasoning behind this therapy is based on the idea that certain brain areas are involved in regulating different bodily functions and behaviors. When these areas are not functioning correctly, it can lead to various symptoms and disorders. Brain stimulation therapy aims to improve their functioning and alleviate the associated symptoms by stimulating these areas with electrical or magnetic fields.

Following are some examples of brain stimulation therapies for depression.

Transcranial Magnetic Stimulation (TMS)

TMS is a non-invasive therapy where magnetic fields are generated by a coil placed on the scalp, which produces small electrical currents that can activate or inhibit the brain cells beneath it.

During a TMS session, the patient sits comfortably in a chair while the coil is placed on their scalp. The coil produces a series of brief magnetic pulses that pass through the skull and stimulate the brain cells beneath it. The stimulation can target specific brain areas associated with particular symptoms or disorders.

Vagus Nerve Stimulation (VNS)

VNS is a type of therapy that uses electrical impulses to stimulate the vagus nerve, which connects the brain to various organs in the body, including the heart, lungs, and digestive system.

During VNS therapy, a small device is implanted under the skin in the chest and connected to the vagus nerve. The device delivers regular electrical impulses to the nerve, which aids in regulating many bodily functions and activities. VNS is used to treat depression because it's believed to affect neurotransmitters in the brain and modulate the activity of various regions involved in regulating mood and pain.

Electroconvulsive Therapy (ECT)

ECT is a treatment in which an electric current is passed through the brain to cause a short seizure to alleviate symptoms associated with depression.

During an ECT session, the patient is given anesthesia to minimize discomfort and prevent muscle spasms. Electrodes are placed on the scalp, and a controlled electrical current is passed through the brain, inducing a seizure that lasts for a few seconds.

ECT is usually only advised for severe cases of depression. Although it's seen as an effective treatment option, it can also have side effects, such as temporary memory loss and confusion.

Light therapy

Light therapy, also known as bright light therapy, is a treatment that involves exposure to a bright light source. Research has shown that it can effectively treat Seasonal Affective Disorder (page 24) and other types of depression.[11,12].

During light therapy, an individual sits in front of a light box that emits a bright, white light for a prescribed amount each day, usually in the morning. The light mimics natural outdoor light, which can help regulate the body's circadian rhythm and boost mood. Although light treatment is generally considered safe, some people may experience side effects such as headaches, eye strain, or nausea.

Exercise/Physical Activity

Studies show exercise as an effective treatment for depression.[13,14,15] Here are some of the reasons why.

- Exercise has been found to increase the release of endorphins and other feel-good chemicals in the brain, which can help to reduce feelings of sadness, anxiety, and stress. These chemicals act as natural antidepressants, improving mood, reducing tension, and promoting relaxation.
- Physical activities can help to reduce the levels of inflammatory markers in the body. (Research suggests that inflammation may play a role in the development of depression).
- Exercise may help boost self-esteem and self-confidence, which can be especially good for persons with feelings of worthlessness or low self-esteem.
- Exercise routines can provide a sense of structure, which can be helpful for individuals with depression who may struggle with motivation and energy levels.
- Physical activity can distract from negative thoughts and feelings, enabling people to focus on something positive and enjoyable.

Psychotherapy

Psychotherapy, or *talk therapy*, involves consulting with a mental health professional to explore and address underlying issues contributing to depression.

The efficacy of psychotherapy in treating depression can vary depending on the individual and the type of therapy used. However, it's considered a highly effective treatment option for depression[16,17] in part because it provides a safe and supportive environment in which individuals can explore their thoughts and feelings. In one study, psychotherapy was found effective in treating depression with an average effect size of 0.70, which indicates a moderate to significant treatment effect.[18]

During a session, the therapist and patient engage in a dialogue to explore the patient's thoughts, feelings, and behaviors. The therapist then uses various techniques to help the patient gain insight into their issues, develop coping strategies, and make positive changes in their life.

Following are some of the types of psychotherapy used to treat depression.

Emotion-Focused Therapy (EFT)

EFT is a form of psychotherapy that focuses on helping individuals understand and regulate their emotions. The goal is to help people understand the emotional experiences that underpin their beliefs, behaviors, and relationships. Standard techniques used in EFT include guided imagery, role-playing, and emotion-focused journaling.

Interpersonal Psychotherapy (IPT)

IPT focuses on addressing interpersonal issues and improving interpersonal relationships. The goal is to help people identify and resolve problems related to their relationships with others, which may be contributing to their mental health problems.

During an IPT session, the therapist works with the individual to identify problematic interpersonal patterns and behaviors, such as difficulty communicating or maintaining healthy boundaries. The therapist then helps the individual develop new skills and strategies for improving their relationships and addressing interpersonal problems. Standard techniques used in IPT include role-playing, communication exercises, and problem-solving strategies.

Cognitive Behavior Therapy (CBT)

CBT aims to recognize and change problematic thought patterns and behaviors. The objective is to help individuals develop more positive and adaptive ways of thinking and behaving, leading to improvements in mental health.

During a session, the therapist works with the individual to identify negative or unhelpful thoughts and beliefs and challenge and reframe them more positively. The therapist may also work with the individual to develop coping strategies and behavioral techniques for managing symptoms of mental health conditions. Standard techniques used in CBT include cognitive restructuring, exposure therapy, and behavioral activation.

Dialectical Behavior Therapy (DBT)

DBT is a form of psychotherapy that combines elements of CBT and mindfulness practices. The goal is to help individuals understand their current circumstances, learn mindfulness, develop coping strategies for dealing with difficult situations, manage intense emotions, and learn skills to improve relationships. DBT is what we will cover in great detail in this book.

Over the years, I have tried various therapies and found DBT the most helpful. I believe it effectively combines different types of therapies, and the techniques involved are relatable and doable in real life.

With DBT, I finally became the well-adjusted adult I am today. I hope it helps you as much as it has helped me.

Chapter Highlights:

- **Depression**, or major depressive disorder (MDD), is a mood disorder that affects how your emotions, thoughts, and behavior. It is characterized by persistent feelings of sadness and despair, and loss of interest in activities one previously enjoyed.
- **Depression Possible Causes**: Genetics, brain chemistry, life events, medical conditions, substance abuse, hormonal changes, and medication.
- **Depression Symptoms**: Constant feelings of sadness, loss of interest or pleasure in formally enjoyable activities, fluctuations in appetite or weight loss, sleeping problems, fatigue or loss of energy, feelings of guilt or low self-esteem, psychomotor agitation or retardation, difficulty handling intense emotions, isolation, thoughts of self-harm and suicide ideation.
- **Depression Types**: Major Depressive Disorder (MDD), Persistent Depressive Disorder (PDD), Postpartum Depression (PPD), Seasonal Affective Disorder, Psychotic Depression, and Bipolar Disorder.
- **Depression Recommended Treatments**: Antidepressants, brain stimulation therapies, bright light therapy, exercise, and psychotherapy.

Living with Depression

> *"Depression is like a heaviness that you can't ever escape.*
> *It crushes down on you, making even the smallest things like*
> *tying your shoes or chewing on toast seem like a twenty-mile*
> *hike uphill." – Unknown*

Whenever I get asked about how it feels to suffer from depression, I get a bit tongue-tied.

How do you tell someone that even simple things like getting out of bed or brushing their teeth take so much energy and concentration? How do you describe to someone this constant lack of interest in doing anything at all? How do you explain this unrelenting darkness that hangs over you and that you have absolutely no way—or desire—to see beyond it? How do you make someone understand that you don't want to "participate"?

I knew my OCD was behind my obsessions (constant intrusive, unwanted thoughts) around self-harm and death. But even though I didn't want to take my own life, I had zero interest in life. (That's the depression talking.)

My anxiety disorder didn't help, either. For example, when my fears and worries kick in that I can't function properly, I'd start to feel a sense of worthlessness. Thoughts like, *"Why can't I just do this?"*, *"Why am I always panicking?"* or *"Why am I always sweating and trembling?"* made me criticize myself harshly, lowering my self-esteem. These thoughts pushed me further down the depression hole.

Understanding how the depression *caused* and *affected* so many facets of my life was the first step in my recovery. I hope the following sections do the same for you.

Depression and the Brain

As previously discussed, depression is widely believed to be caused by abnormalities in brain chemistry. However, during depressive episodes, *further changes* happen to our brains.

Brain Shrinkage

Shrinkage is one of the most prevalent alterations in a depressed person's brain, particularly in the hippocampus, thalamus, frontal cortex, and prefrontal cortex. The gravity of brain shrinkage is determined by the duration and degree of one's depression.

Research shows that people with depression lose gray matter volume (GMV).[19] This loss happens because *cortisol* prevents brain cells from growing. The graver the episode, the more GMV one loses. Since most of our nerve cells are in our GMV, slowed brain cell formation could negatively impact our ability to think and reason.

While high cortisol levels cause certain brain parts to shrink, the amygdala grows. Because the amygdala regulates emotions, this could result in difficulty sleeping, mood swings, and other issues.

Brain Inflammation

Research shows that depression is linked to cerebral inflammation.[20] Experts don't know if depression causes brain inflammation or if it's the other way around, but researchers believe the two are linked.

Inflammation in the brain can lead to changes in the way that neurons communicate with each other. Changes in neurotransmitter levels, such as *serotonin* and *dopamine*, which are important in mood regulation, may also occur.

When neurons and neurotransmitters die, the brain will likely shrink and lose its ability to change as a person ages. (This is called *neuroplasticity*.) Since new neurons and neurotransmitters have a more challenging time growing, a person suffering from depression may develop cognitive problems.

Limited Oxygen Intake

People suffering from MDD may take in less oxygen.[21] It's believed that depression changes how you breathe, leading to a lack of oxygen (*hypoxia*).

Hypoxia can impair cognitive performance. This can result in decision-making problems, losing motor skills, and experiencing bouts of forgetfulness.

Depression and the Body

Depression is a mental health disorder that can harm our physical health.

If you remember, one of the symptoms of depression is fluctuations in appetite or weight. Overeating can lead to weight gain and obesity-related conditions like type 2 diabetes. Undereating can make your body go into starvation mode, leading to low blood pressure, fertility troubles, heart problems, etc.

Research has also shown a connection between depression and the immune system.[22,23] This may be because depression can increase inflammation in the body, impairing the immune system's ability to fight off infections.

In addition, depression can change how the immune system functions. For example, depression has been linked to lower production of T cells and natural killer cells, which are important for fighting infections and cancer. Depression has also been associated with increased production of pro-inflammatory cytokines, which can contribute to chronic inflammation and other health problems.

Depression and Relationships

Depression can negatively impact your relationships.[24] As I mentioned before, my alienation at school made me withdraw from society even more. So, not only did I miss out on opportunities to meet new people and form new relationships, but it also made things worse with my family, with whom I already had issues.

People suffering from depression have *difficulty expressing their thoughts and feelings*, which can lead to a breakdown in communication with loved ones. In the Chinese culture, we don't have emotional expression; we have emotional suppression, so I was already used to NOT discussing problems with my family. However, when I left home and started to make friends and even get into relationships, it was tough to discuss, let alone try to describe, what I felt. This led to a lot of failed relationships.

The depressive symptom of *lack of interest in doing anything* is also detrimental to relationships. Of course, people who care about us want to spend meaningful time with us. Suppose all we want to do is stay in bed because we don't have the energy or the interest to do anything. In that case, this can be interpreted as a lack of interest in them. Who wants to be in a relationship where your partner is not invested in you or interested in the things you like?

There are also a lot of *negative thinking patterns* with depression, which can cause individuals to interpret their partner's words or behavior negatively. This can lead to misunderstandings and further strain on the relationship.

This is what Dennis[†], a reader, had to say: *"I didn't know I was depressed until it was too late. I lost my job six years ago. First, I was just a grumpy person to be around with. Then there was a lot of anger, which I directed to everyone around me. I wouldn't get physical with anyone. I was the passive-aggressive type.*

I would apply for jobs but wouldn't get them, so I lost my sense of humor along the way, and the grumpiness and anger were replaced by self-doubt, which I dared not admit to anyone.

After that, I lost interest in trying to get a job altogether. It cost too much energy, and looking back, I guess I was trying to escape failure. If I didn't apply for anything, no one could say "No" to me, right?

I started to avoid people because I didn't want to be asked how the "job hunting" was going. My wife was the sole breadwinner by this time, and my self-esteem just went down the drain. I felt enormous guilt but at the same time... I wouldn't do anything about it. We started to get into many fights; our sex life became nonexistent, and we hardly even looked at each other.

One day, my wife told me she was taking the kids and staying with her parents for a while. I knew she was going to ask for a divorce sooner or later. I would.

The first week they were gone, I couldn't eat or sleep. At this point, I felt there was nothing left to live for anymore, and I started to have "bad thoughts." When I found myself planning the exact steps to carry out my "bad thoughts," I knew it was time to talk to someone. Either that, or I would do what I shouldn't do. So, I called my sister. She's a medical doctor, and she was the one who booked my first consultation with a psychiatrist friend she knew.

[†] *Named changed for privacy.*

I was diagnosed with MDD, and thankfully, I'm better now. Sadly, I still lost my family. The good thing is I'm on good terms with my ex-wife. She even joined one of my sessions, and that was the first time I heard how my depression made her feel that she carried everything and everyone on her shoulders. My negative thoughts and behavior were also starting to bring her down, and that's when she knew she had to go. I don't blame her one bit.

Depression in Women

Although the above story is from a male perspective, research shows that women are more likely to develop depression than men.[25] Following are some of the risk factors that have been researched that may explain this.

Hormones

Women experience hormonal changes throughout life, including puberty, menstruation, pregnancy, and menopause. Men also experience hormonal changes during puberty but don't go through menstruation, pregnancy, and menopause. That alone increases the chances of women developing depression more than men. Why is this relevant? Hormonal changes affect brain chemistry and mood, affecting the risk of developing depression.

Societal and Cultural Factors

Biology isn't the only thing that increases the development of depression in women. Females often face social and cultural stressors that men don't face.

Gender inequality at work. Women often get paid less than men for the same work. In the US, data from the Pew Research Center reveals that in 2022, *"women earned an average of 82% of what men earned."*[26]. Women are also more likely to be a victim of violence in the workplace.[27] However, it's important to note that men are less likely to report such experiences than women.

Gender inequality at home. Working women feel more pressure to focus on their responsibilities at home than working men. This means that despite a full workload, women still care for many things at home. Working or not, women also care for others (e.g., parents, extended family, etc.) more than men.

Differences in Coping Mechanisms

Men and women may also differ in coping mechanisms for stress and adversity. Women may be more likely to ruminate and internalize stress. In contrast, men are likelier to adopt a more problem-solving, distracting coping style to help them through difficult times.[28]

Rumination, or the tendency to focus on negative thoughts and feelings, has been linked to developing and maintaining depression.[29,30]

Chapter Highlights:

- **Depression and the brain.** One of the causes of MDD is abnormalities in brain chemistry. This section discusses how the brain is physically altered during depressive episodes.
- **Depression and the body.** Depression is detrimental to physical health. It can weaken the immune system and cause various health problems.
- **Depression and relationships.** This section explores how MDD can negatively affect even the healthiest of relationships.
- **Depression in women.** Depression is twice more likely to occur in women than in men. This section discusses the various factors that influence this.

What is Dialectical Behavior Therapy?

"You don't have to be perfect to begin the healing process. You just have to be willing to start." - Unknown

Dialectical Behavior Therapy (DBT) is a type of therapy that combines cognitive-behavioral techniques (CBT) with mindfulness practices. Psychologist Dr. Marsha Linehan initially developed it in the late 1980s to treat individuals with borderline personality disorder (BPD).

As far as psychotherapies go, DBT is actually considered "new." However, it's been so effective that today, it's used to treat various mental health conditions, including depression.

When I first learned about DBT, I was fascinated by the fact that Dr. Linehan suffered from BPD. It made me wonder if DBT is so effective as a mental health treatment because the person who developed it herself suffered from a mental health condition.

Dr. Linehan was born in 1943 in Tulsa, Oklahoma, and experienced significant emotional turmoil as a child and adolescent. In the 1960s, she was admitted to the *Institute of Living*, a psychiatric clinic, because of "extreme social withdrawal" symptoms. At the clinic, she constantly engaged in self-harming behaviors and demonstrated suicidal behavior.

In the 1960s, BPD was not yet officially diagnosable as a disorder. (It would be in the 1980s.) As such, Dr. Linehan was misdiagnosed with schizophrenia, subjected to electroconvulsive therapy, and prescribed antipsychotic medication. Of course, since she did NOT have schizophrenia, these methods did not work to treat her symptoms. After two years, Dr. Linehan was released from the Institute of Living but was still unwell.

Despite her challenges, Dr. Linehan earned her Ph.D. in clinical psychology from Loyola University Chicago and began her career as a researcher and clinician. She later became interested in working with individuals with BPD. During this time, she noticed that traditional therapies were ineffective in treating their symptoms. In response, Dr. Linehan began to develop DBT, which incorporates *mindfulness practices* and *skills training* to help individuals regulate their emotions and improve their relationships.

Another thing that was ground breaking about Dr. Linehan's therapy was the application of *dialectics*.

Dialectics

Dialectics is a word that comes from the ancient Greek philosopher Heraclitus. He believed that change is constant and that reality comprises opposing forces always working together. In psychology, dialectics is a way of thinking and solving problems that involve recognizing and balancing different ideas or points of view.

So, dialectics is the art of balancing opposing viewpoints to resolve conflict. In DBT, the dialectical approach involves balancing acceptance of the present moment with a desire for change and growth to cope or heal from mental health problems.

The following are a few exercises[31] to help you get used to dialectical thinking. Please remember that dialectics is an exercise in seeing all sides. Experiencing problems or crises doesn't mean we're stuck in this state. At the same time, seeing another side of our problems doesn't invalidate how difficult or painful the situation is to you.

Worksheet: Wrong AND Right

When going through something painful or difficult, it's easy to focus on what's wrong while ignoring the other side of the debate, which is what is going right. Asking what's going right or good, no matter how minor, provides a different perspective and balance.

What's wrong?	What's going right?
Example: My best friend of nearly a decade has just stopped talking to me, and I don't know why. I feel so confused, betrayed, and alone.	*Example: I have other friends who continue to love and support me.*
Your turn:	Your turn:

Worksheet: The Silver Lining

It may not feel or appear this way when you have a significant problem or crisis, but not many things in life are *all good* or *all bad*. Consider whether there is a silver lining in what you're going through. Problems, even tragedies, can reveal opportunities.

The Situation	The Silvering Lining
Example: After 26 years of marriage, my partner and I decided to get a divorce.	*Example: I've always wanted to pursue art. I used to be good with painting but gave it up when the kids came along. Now the kids are pursuing their dreams, maybe now's the chance for me to pursue mine.*
Your turn:	Your turn:

Why DBT for Depression?

Although initially developed for people with BPD, DBT has been found to be highly effective in treating other mental health disorders.[32,33,34] This is not surprising given that DBT was originally established with an emphasis on *emotion regulation*, which is directly linked to one's ability to manage the mood changes associated with depression.

Another reason DBT is particularly beneficial, in my opinion, is that it's not all "theory." The exercises really helped me learn and use the skills in my daily life. You're physically working your way through your mental health issues. I was literally working through my mental health struggles as I tried the exercises.

DBT Core Concepts

In DBT, we need to recognise and balance two opposing viewpoints: Acceptance and Change.

Radical Acceptance

Acceptance refers to acknowledging and embracing one's emotions and experiences without judgment. It involves letting go of the idea that some emotions are "good" or "bad" and instead recognizing that all emotions are valid and serve a purpose.

The statement that "all emotions are valid and serve a purpose" has been very healing to me.

One of the main problems with mental health problems is that people, intentionally or unintentionally, frequently invalidate us. People can "see" my OCD so that they can understand it somehow. However, when it comes to my anxiety and depression, I've received comments like "just get over it," "toughen up," "why can't you just be more positive?", "stop feeling sorry for yourself; it's not that bad," and many others. I'd heard these comments so often that I started to feel bad and sometimes even doubted my emotions. With DBT, I learned that my emotions and experiences are valid and that I should accept them for what they are.

In DBT, Dr. Linehan uses the term **Radical Acceptance** because it involves fully and completely accepting reality as it is in the present moment, without judgment or resistance. It's the practice of accepting what we cannot change and letting go of the struggle to control or resist it.

People with mental health disorders struggle with difficult or distressing emotions, experiences, or circumstances. However, instead of fighting or trying to escape these realities, Radical Acceptance encourages us to embrace them fully and find a way to move forward positively.

I'll be the first to say that Radical Acceptance can be difficult, especially in particularly painful or challenging situations. Sometimes, I like to use this analogy: the bad stomach ache.

When we have a terrible tummy problem, what do we physically do? We bend over and clutch our stomachs. We may ask ourselves: *What did I eat? What did I drink? How did I get this?* We might even blame someone for our troubles: *If only Tim had not forced that spicy dish on me!* We might blame ourselves: *Why did I have to drink/eat so late last night?!* Next, we might start to worry: *What if this doesn't clear by tomorrow? I have a critical presentation in the morning.* If you suffer from an anxiety disorder like me, your thoughts might even go so far as... *what if this is cancer?*

In all of the above statements and scenarios, we are, in effect, *nurturing* our stomach ache (the problem). When we give our problems so much attention, we *stay* in that state of mind and prolong our suffering.

Radical Acceptance helps you to let go of your emotional suffering and focus on taking action to improve your situation.

So in the above "bad stomach ache" example, you forego all your contemplations and ruminations and go straight to making things better for yourself (e.g., take an antacid, drink plenty of water, rest, drink ginger tea, etc.)

There are also a few misconceptions about Radical Acceptance. I hope the following helps clarify this concept for you.

Radical Acceptance IS NOT	Radical Acceptance IS
NOT agreement, approval, or consent. You're not okay with the situation; you accept that the situation is happening or has happened.	
NOT giving up or giving in. You're not saying you don't want things to improve. Accepting NOW doesn't mean you want the situation to stay that way.	
NOT inaction. You're not saying you're okay with whatever life throws at you. You accept what happened because it's in the past; *taking action* belongs to the future.	*Accepting that a situation exists.*
NOT avoidance. You're not avoiding or ignoring your emotions or problems. You acknowledge and accept them to find ways to address them effectively.	
NOT about others. Your reality is yours alone, so you don't accept for others, only for yourself.	

Worksheet: Radical Acceptance

Radical Acceptance is reality acceptance. So for your first exercise, please write your current reality inside the circle below. Just write down whatever comes to mind. Remember, all your emotions and experiences are valid.

Examples: (1) I'm lonely. (2) I'm so tired. (3) I'm not interested in anything. (4) No, I don't want to "participate." (5) I'm grieving.

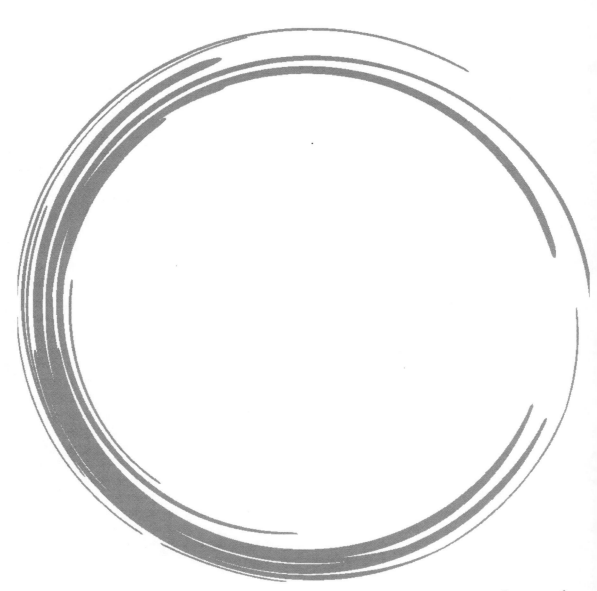

Change

Change is the opposing viewpoint in DBT. It's the part that balances Acceptance and refers to the active process of developing new skills and behaviors to feel better and improve your situation.

If you think change is hard, you're right. Humans are hardwired to resist change. One of the primary reasons is that change often requires us to step out of our comfort zones and confront the unknown. We may also worry about losing what we have or fear we cannot handle "new."

Another reason we may resist change is that it requires effort and energy. Change often involves breaking old habits, learning new skills, and developing new ways of thinking. This can be difficult and time-consuming and requires a willingness to be patient and persistent.

Lastly, humans are social creatures who often rely on the support of others. When we try to change our lives, we may face resistance from others who are not ready or willing to see us change or change with us. This can make us feel isolated or unsupported, undermining our motivation to change.

So, if you resist change, that's okay; that's a normal reaction.

At the start, I, too, had issues with "change" regarding my mental health problems. It made me feel that I was somehow the one at fault and to blame for my circumstances. But DBT taught me that I need to change because the "methods" I was using to deal with my mental health problems weren't working or weren't working as well as they used to. And why should I keep using them if they're not or no longer working?

Imagine having a favorite sweater. It's gotten two sizes too small and doesn't keep you warm anymore. Why grab it every time it gets cold?

Worksheet: Desire to Change

Start cultivating a change mindset by writing down a few thoughts on how change can benefit your life. Please don't overthink this. Just write down whatever comes to mind inside the circle below.

Examples: (1) *I'm ready for "new." (2) I'm ready for "different." (3) I'm ready for "better." (4) It's time to be happy again. (5) I'm ready for more people in my life.*

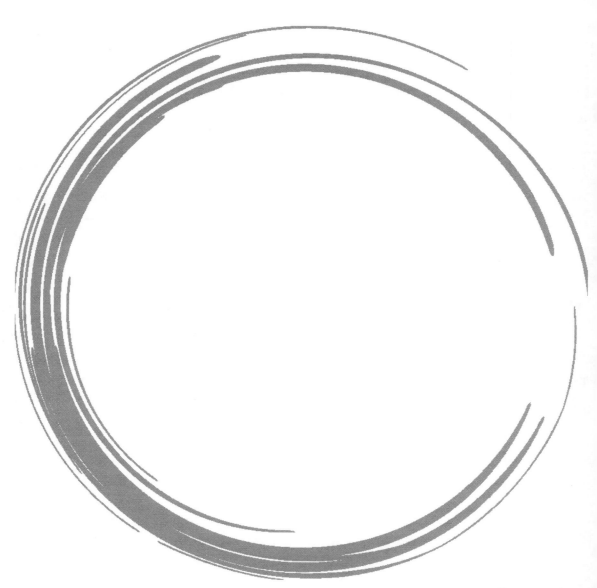

Worksheet: Acceptance and Change

Let's bring Radical Acceptance and Desire to Change together.

RADICAL ACCEPTANCE: Write statements accepting your reality today.

DESIRE TO CHANGE: Write statements expressing your desire to change or how change can benefit your life.

DECLARATION: Acknowledge today and what you want for tomorrow.

RADICAL ACCEPTANCE:	DECLARATION:	DESIRE TO CHANGE:
I'm lonely.	*"I accept who I am today. Life has its ups and downs and I can't control everything that happens. So, I choose not to fight against the things I can't change.*	*I'm ready for "new."*
I'm so tired.		*I'm ready for "different."*
I'm not interested in anything.		*I'm ready for "better."*
I don't want to "participate."	*I also accept that I'm not living my best life now. I don't feel happy or fulfilled living this way. So I'm opening myself to change. I'm going to give myself the opportunity to grow and find happiness and inner peace."*	*It's time to be happy again.*
I'm in pain.		*I want to smile again.*
I don't have hope.		*I want friends.*

Now, it is your turn!

RADICAL ACCEPTANCE: DECLARATION: **DESIRE TO CHANGE:**

DBT Core Skills

DBT comprises four core skills: *Mindfulness, Distress Tolerance, Emotion Regulation*, and *Interpersonal Effectiveness.*

Acceptance is enabled by Mindfulness and Distress Tolerance skills, whereas **Change** is accomplished through Emotion Regulation and Interpersonal Effectiveness skills.

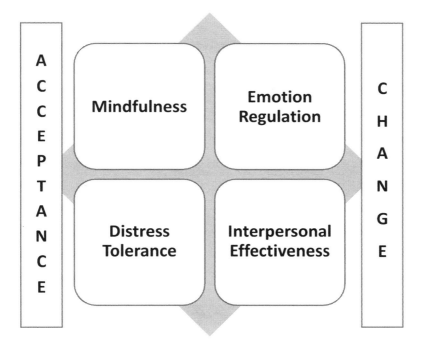

Mindfulness

"Mindfulness is simply being aware of what is happening right now without wishing it were different; enjoying the pleasant without holding on when it changes (which it will); being with the unpleasant without fearing it will always be this way (which it won't)." - James Baraz

Mindfulness is being fully present in the present moment, fully aware of your surroundings, thoughts, and feelings. It involves paying attention to your experiences without judgment and with a sense of curiosity and openness.

It's the practice of being fully engaged in the moment. You're not in the past or in the future. You're just in NOW.

Mindfulness is a core component of DBT because it helps us develop greater awareness of our thoughts, feelings, and behaviors. It also cultivates greater acceptance and non-judgment of our experiences. Practicing mindfulness allows us to observe our thoughts and emotions without getting caught up in them.

As you learn more about DBT and this book, you will also realize that mindfulness is the basis for all the other skills you will learn.

Mindfulness was not unknown to me, but I never practiced it. I didn't think I could do it, let alone think of it as a way to get better. I thought, *"How can I practice "mindfulness" when my mind is too troubled by the mental health problems I already have?"*

Of course, with DBT, I realized that I had it backwards. Mindfulness is a way to quiet my mind to get a grip on whatever's happening. For this reason, I like to call mindfulness a "mental pause." It's that ability to take a moment to focus and be aware of yourself and your surroundings. Today, mindfulness is part of my daily life.

Often, people think that mindfulness and meditation are the same. They may be related, but they have some essential differences.

Mindfulness is a quality or character trait. A mindful person is someone who can easily be present in the moment. They're aware of their thoughts, feelings, and sensations without judgment. They can observe external stimuli and their internal experiences without getting caught up in them or reacting impulsively.

Meditation is a practice that involves setting aside time to intentionally focus on a particular object or activity, such as the breath or a mantra. Meditation aims to train the mind to be more focused and attentive and to develop greater awareness of one's thoughts and feelings.

So, meditation is a tool for developing mindfulness, but mindfulness is something that we can cultivate and practice in all aspects of our lives.

The Breath

At first glance, "breathing" may seem so basic. After all, we've been doing it since the day we were born. However, it's important to note that most people, especially those suffering from mental health disorders or medical conditions, are "shallow breathers."

Shallow breathing (a.k.a. chest breathing) takes fast, short breaths that only fill a tiny area of the lungs. This form of breathing frequently involves using the chest muscles rather than the diaphragm, the primary breathing muscle. Shallow breathing can negatively affect our health and well-being. It can reduce oxygen intake and increase stress and fatigue. This is why when we have a mental health episode, it's easy to end up hyperventilating or experience shortness of breath.

So, our usual breathing pattern does NOT promote mindfulness. We need to learn how to breathe deeper and with more intention. We do this through breathing exercises.

Breathing exercises can effectively cultivate mindfulness because they require you to focus on your breath, which can help quiet your mind and bring your awareness to the present moment. Focusing on your breath will make you less likely to focus on distracting thoughts or worries.

Here are a few ways in which breathing exercises can help you be more mindful:

1. **Breath awareness.** Focusing on your breath can help you become more aware of the physical sensations in your body and the present moment. As you inhale and exhale, notice how the air moves in and out of your nostrils, the rise and fall of your chest and belly, and your body sensations as you breathe.

2. **Centering.** Deep breathing exercises can help you feel more centered and grounded, which can help you feel calmer and more focused. Taking slow, deliberate, deep breaths can slow your heart rate and reduce stress and anxiety.

3. **Attention training.** When you focus on your breath, you're training your attention to be present in the moment. This can help you develop greater awareness and concentration, which can help you be more mindful in other areas of your life.

4. **Emotional regulation.** Breathing exercises can help you regulate your emotions by slowing your breathing and calming your nervous system.[35] By regulating your breath, you can reduce distress, anxiety, and overwhelm and cultivate feelings of calm and relaxation. (We'll cover Emotion Regulation in detail on page 106.)

On the following pages are several exercises that will help you develop the core DBT skill of mindfulness. We'll start with breathing exercises (beginner to advanced) and end with various types of meditation practices.

Note: During your breathing exercises, try to observe your breath. Please note how it feels in your nose, throat, chest, and stomach. If your thoughts wander (and they will!), gently bring them back to your breath. If it helps you focus, use the phrases "breathing in" and "breathing out" as you do the exercises.

Worksheet: Belly Breathing

Belly Breathing (a.k.a. diaphragmatic breathing) promotes relaxation and stress reduction. It's a great beginner exercise for shallow breathers. The following are the steps for belly breathing.

1. Sit down comfortably or lie down on your bed.
2. Put one hand on your belly and the other on your chest.
3. Inhale gently through your nose, allowing your belly to expand like a balloon. (Your chest should remain relatively still.)
4. Exhale slowly through your mouth, letting your belly deflate like a balloon. (Try to let all the air out of your lungs.)
5. Continue to breathe this way, focusing on the sensation of your belly rising and falling like gentle ocean waves with each breath.

Ensure that you're breathing deeply from your diaphragm rather than shallowly from your chest. You can also practice this technique with closed eyes, visualizing a peaceful scene to enhance relaxation. Gradually increase the duration of your belly breaths as you become more comfortable with the technique.

Worksheet: Equal Breathing (Sama Vritti)

This breathing technique is about equal inhalations and exhalations to improve focus and promote calmness.

1. Lie on your bed or mat, or find a comfortable seated position.
2. Close your eyes and take a few deep breaths to relax your body.
3. **Inhale** slowly and deeply through your nose for a count of four

4. **Exhale** slowly and thoroughly through your nose for a count of four.

5. Continue inhaling and exhaling through your nose for a few more cycles, maintaining an even count for each inhale and exhale.

As you become more comfortable with the practice, you can gradually increase the length of your inhales and exhales to a count of five, six, or more.

Worksheet: Box Breathing

In the previous exercises, you were inhaling and expelling your breaths. This time, we'll add holding your breath to the exercise.

1. Lie on your bed or mat, or find a comfortable seated position.
2. Close your eyes and take a few deep breaths to relax your body.
3. **Inhale** through your nose for four counts. Imagine drawing air all the way into your belly.

4. **Hold** your breath for four counts.

5. **Exhale** gently and completely through your mouth for four counts, releasing all the air from your lungs.

6. **Hold** your breath for four counts before starting the next inhale.

Repeat this pattern for several minutes, gradually increasing the duration of each breath and holding as you become more comfortable with the technique. The goal is to create a slow, steady breathing rhythm that helps calm your mind and body.

Worksheet: 4-7-8 Breathing

4-7-8 Breathing is an advanced breathing technique that promotes deep relaxation. In this exercise, you'll hold and exhale your breath longer than your inhalations. This controlled breathing technique is also believed to decrease symptoms of depression and anxiety.[36]

1. Lie on your bed or mat, or find a comfortable seated position.
2. Close your eyes and take a few deep breaths to relax your body.
3. INHALE for 4 counts through your nose.

4. HOLD YOUR BREATH for 7 counts...

5. EXHALE for 8 counts through your mouth.

6. Do steps 3-5 for at least four cycles.

When you're finished, release your hand and sit quietly, noticing any sensations in your body and mind.

Worksheet: Nadi Shodhana (Alternate Nostril Breathing)

Nadi Shodhana is a yogic breathing technique that aims to balance the flow of energy (*prana*) in the body and calm the mind. The purpose of this breathing practice is to purify and balance the *nadis*, which are the subtle energy channels in the body according to yoga philosophy.

1. Sit in a comfortable seated position, either on the floor or in a chair, with your spine straight and your shoulders relaxed.
2. Place your left hand on your left knee, palm facing up, and bring your right hand to your face.
3. With your right hand, bring your index finger and middle finger to rest between your eyebrows, and use your thumb to close your right nostril.
4. Inhale deeply through your left nostril for a count of four, then use your ring finger to close your left nostril.
5. Hold your breath for a count of four.
6. Release your right nostril and exhale slowly for a count of eight.
7. Inhale deeply through your right nostril for a count of four, then use your thumb to close your right nostril.
8. Hold your breath for a count of four.
9. Release your left nostril and exhale slowly for a count of eight.
10. This completes one cycle of Nadi Shodhana. Repeat steps 4-9 for several more rounds, alternating nostrils with each cycle.

As you become more comfortable with the practice, you can gradually increase the duration of each breath and hold.

When you're finished, release your hand and sit quietly, noticing any sensations in your body and mind.

Worksheet: Mindful Breathing Reflection

It would be best if you made time for breathing exercises to develop mindfulness. To get the most out of the previous exercises, it also helps to do a bit of reflection. Following are a few questions for you.

1. **WHAT** is the best time for you to do breathing exercises?

   Example: In the morning, just after I wake up and before I go to work.

   Answer: _____

2. **WHERE** is the best place for you to do breathing exercises?

   Example: at my attic, I created a small "ME" space there

   Answer: _____

3. **WHICH** breathing exercise was easy, and why?

   Example: Belly Breathing because I didn't have to think about breath counts.

   Answer: _____

4. **WHICH** breathing exercise was challenging, and why?

   Example: Nadi Shodhana because I needed to get used to the technique of alternate nostril breathing.

   Answer: _____

5. **AFTER** a breathing exercise, reflect on how you felt? For example, were you more relaxed, less stressed, or less anxious?

   Answer: _____

   _____

   _____

   _____

   _____

Worksheet: Meditation 101

Meditation is a mindfulness practice to help you focus on the present moment without judgment or distraction. For beginners, here is a step-by-step instruction for basic meditation.

1. Choose a quiet, comfortable area where you will not be bothered. Place your feet flat on the floor and sit on a cushion or chair with your back straight. Place your hands on your knees or your lap for support.

2. Set a 5-10 minute timer. This will assist you in remaining focused and committed to your practice.

3. Take a few deep breaths and close your eyes. Exhale slowly through your lips and inhale slowly through your nose.

4. Begin to concentrate on your breathing. Take note of the sensation of air passing in and out of your nose and the rise and fall of your belly. Allow your breathing to be as natural and effortless as possible.

5. When your mind wanders (which it will!), gently bring it back to your breath. To stay focused, employ a mental anchor, such as the words "inhale" or "exhale."

6. Any ideas or sensations that arise should be noted, but they should not be allowed to consume you. Merely observe them without judgment or distraction, then return your focus to breathing.

7. Take a few deep breaths and slowly open your eyes when your timer goes off. Reflect on how you're feeling, and take note of any changes (mental, emotional, or physical).

Worksheet: Loving Kindness Meditation

Loving Kindness Meditation (LKM) is a time to promote kindness and compassion to yourself and others. Here is a step-by-step guide:

1. Lie on your bed or mat, or find a comfortable seated position.
2. Let yourself relax by taking a few deep breaths.
3. Once you feel centered, start focusing on a feeling of inner love and kindness. Next, silently offer a simple statement of kindness to yourself.

   Examples:

   May I be content.

   May I be happy today.

   I'll remember that I'm a good person.

   I'm doing my best.

   I'm a good person

   What statements of love and kindness do you want to say to yourself?

   _____

   _____

   _____

   _____

   _____

4. As you channel kindness to yourself, imagine being encircled by a warm, loving glow. Feel the love and compassion you're offering yourself; you deserve it.
5. Next, think of someone you care about and want to extend love and kindness to.

   I want to extend love and kindness to:

   Example: my youngest brother

   _____

I want to say:

Example: I know you're also going through tough times now. I wish you peace of mind.

_____

_____

_____

6. Think of someone you feel *neutral* about and want to extend love and kindness to.

I want to extend love and kindness to:

Example: my elderly next-door neighbor

_____

I want to say:

Example: May you be healthy and pain-free.

_____

_____

_____

7. Think of someone you may *dislike* and extend thoughts of love and kindness to them. (Note: It's okay to skip this step if you're not ready.)

I want to extend love and kindness to:

Example: my ex

_____

I want to say:

Example: I wish you contentment.

_____

_____

_____

8. As you do steps 5-7, feel love and compassion pouring towards them as you offer your statements of love and kindness.

9. If you're ready, extend love and kindness to all beings, including animals and plants. Consider warm, loving light pouring from you to yourself and others. If you're new to LKM, you might find it weird to extend love and kindness to all plants and animals. That's okay. You don't have to if you don't want to. However, please note that animals and plants are also living things, and extending love and kindness to them is just a way of expressing gratitude.

   Examples:
   I extend love and kindness to my pet cat Mia. I don't think she knows how much she helps me.
   To my 15-year-old Lady Palm plant. THANK YOU for brightening my space.

   _____

   _____

   _____

   _____

   _____

10. When you're done, open your eyes slowly and take a few deep breaths. Take some time to reflect on how you're feeling.

Even if it's only for a few minutes, try practicing Loving Kindness meditation daily. Over time, you'll grow in your love, compassion, and empathy for yourself and others.

Worksheet: Walking Meditation

Meditation is not always about keeping still. Mindfulness is about being present in the moment—any moment. So the following is an exercise on how to be mindful while doing the simple act of walking.

1. Find a safe and quiet place to walk, preferably a route without many distractions. It could be a garden, a park, or any other place where you can walk peacefully.
2. Take a few deep breaths and momentarily stand still to calm your body and mind.
3. Slowly put one foot in front of the other and start to walk. Keep your eyes looking forward and stand straight, but don't tense up.
4. Pay close attention to your breath or your steps as you walk. You can say "in" and "out" silently as you breathe in and out or "step" and "pause" as you take each step.
5. If your mind starts to wander, that's okay. Bring your thoughts back to your breathing or your steps. Do this over and over if necessary.
   Important: Don't judge yourself for thoughts or things that distract your attention.
6. After focusing on your breath or steps for a few minutes, start paying attention to what is happening around you. Pay attention to the sights, sounds, and smells around you. Be in the moment and avoid getting caught up in anything else.
7. After a few minutes of walking, try to be more aware of other feelings in your body, like how your arms move or how the wind feels on your skin.
8. When you're ready to end the meditation, stop strolling and stand still for a moment. Take a few deep breaths and let yourself feel centered.

Try Walking Meditation for a few minutes each day. Again, don't worry if your mind wanders or you have trouble focusing on just walking. Just keep on trying. Remember, practice makes ~~perfect~~ progress.

Worksheet: Attitude of Gratitude

Gratitude is frequently regarded as a mindfulness practice since it requires us to be fully present and aware of the positive parts of our existence. When we practice gratitude, we focus our attention on what we are thankful for, which can aid in cultivating a sense of appreciation and contentment in the present moment. Here's how to do a gratitude practice exercise.

1. Choose a peaceful and comfortable sitting area where you will not be bothered.
2. Relax your body by taking a few deep breaths.
3. Consider anything in your life for which you are grateful.

This week, I'm grateful for the following:
Examples: the bright, sunny weather that perks up my spirit

_____

_____

_____

Today, I'm grateful for the following:
Examples: the lunch date I had with my best friend

_____

_____

_____

In the past hour, I've been grateful for the following:
Examples: a warm cup of coffee, an encouraging smile from a co-worker

_____

_____

_____

4. Next, pick one thing for which you are thankful. (It could be something from your list above or something else.) Consider WHY you are grateful for it and how it has benefited your life. Be as detailed as you can.

   Example:

   I'm thankful for a good night's sleep.

   Because: I suffer from insomnia so, it's challenging to fall and stay asleep. Last night was the first time in days that I slept the whole night. I actually woke up "energized."

   I'm thankful for:

   _____

   Because:

   _____

   _____

   _____

5. Sit still now and allow yourself to experience the emotions of thankfulness, such as joy, satisfaction, or calm.

6. Repeat step #4 for anything else for which you are grateful. You can do this practice as long as you want, concentrating on anything that makes you grateful.

   I'm thankful for the following:

   _____

   _____

   _____

Because:

_____

_____

_____

Strive to practice gratitude daily by making a mental list or writing things down in a notebook.

"When you come to the end of your rope,
tie a knot and hang on."— Franklin D. Roosevelt

Distress Tolerance refers to the ability to endure and manage difficult emotions and distressing situations. We do this because if we can't tolerate or survive our depression, we might give in to impulses or behaviors that might worsen the situation.

Stress vs. Distress

Stress is a physiological response to a perceived threat or challenge, whether real or imagined. It's a normal part of the body's fight-or-flight response. It's characterized by physical, emotional, and cognitive symptoms such as increased heart rate, sweating, anxiety, and difficulty concentrating.

Distress, however, is a type of stress that occurs when the body's response to a perceived threat or challenge becomes overwhelming or prolonged. It's often described as negative or unpleasant stress (bad stress) characterized by helplessness, hopelessness, and despair.

STRESS	DISTRESS
Infrequent, short-term	Ongoing, prolonged
Motivates you to take positive action	Can be crippling or debilitating, promoting inaction
Can make you better	Can cause problems and illnesses
Something you believe you can overcome	Something you believe you cannot overcome

This is what Kaycee‡, a reader, had to say: "*I can't pinpoint the exact cause for my depression. My mother's side has a history of it, so maybe that's why. However, for as long as I can remember, I've always had a feeling of deep sadness and loneliness inside me.*

I think I've always felt alone because I was the middle child, and the situation at home was always full of tension. My parents often fought and got very loud and aggressive with each other. Broken plates, harsh name-calling, flying clothes out the window, even broken doors—I've seen them too often.

As my brothers grew older, I realized they were doing the same thing. They would fight and get so loud, angry, and aggressive with each other that I would go to my room and lock the door. I don't know if I was escaping them or if I was actually afraid they would go after me. Either way, I guess this was the beginning of my escaping reality.

Two years ago, I lost my business and sunk into the lowest depression I had ever felt. My impulse was to withdraw from everything and everyone. So that's exactly what I did.

I deactivated my social accounts. I didn't answer calls and text messages. I stayed indoors, and I eventually even stopped showering. I just couldn't find any desire or energy to do anything. I had to eat, but even that seemed pointless, so I consumed one meal daily. Eventually, my thoughts turned to ending it all.

One day, though, the door to my condo opened. My brothers told building security that I was "missing," so the building manager opened my door for

---

‡ *Named changed for privacy.*

them. When they saw me, my brothers and I stared at each other. That's the last thing I remember. I woke up in the psych ward.

In one of my therapy sessions, we uncovered a turning point in my last and most debilitating depressive episode. I shouldn't have given in to my impulse to self-isolate when my business went bust.

This is why I value DBT so much. If I'd known how to take a moment to accept my reality and tolerate my distress, maybe I wouldn't have sunk so deep.

It's important to remember that Distress Tolerance skills not only help you avoid harmful and impulsive actions but also help you build resilience and emotional strength to deal with problems and crises in the future.

You see, we cannot escape highly stressful life events. They will happen, and the secret is to learn how to survive them. The exercises that follow will help you do just that.

Worksheet: Turning the Mind

Before you can tolerate a crisis, you must first radically accept that the crisis exists. However, it's human nature to *reject* a situation when things are not going our way.

Turning the Mind is a practice that involves trying, over and over again, to move toward acceptance. Here's what to do when rejecting a situation or fighting reality.

1. **OBSERVE.** Start by noticing HOW you're rejecting something. This can be your thoughts, emotions, physical responses, etc.

   Example: In my head, I'm hearing, "WHY ME?!?" I guess that's me rejecting the situation even though it already happened. My fists are also clenched, so I'm angry right now.

   What are you observing?

   _____

   _____

   _____

2. **COMMIT.** Make a conscious decision to shift your focus away from your emotional and physical reaction(s) and move toward acceptance.

   Example: I'm choosing to turn my mind away from this emotion. This is the situation. It happened, and I cannot go back, so I won't.

   Your turn:

   _____

   _____

   _____

3. **REPEAT**. Observe and commit repeatedly until you feel yourself accepting the situation. (**Tip**: Do <u>Wrong and Right</u> or <u>Silver Lining</u>, pages 44 and 45, respectively.)

4. **PLAN**. Devise a plan to avoid rejecting unpleasant situations in the future.
   Example: Whenever something bad happens, I'll draw myself a bath with my favorite calming scents. I'll wash away my resistance and come out with acceptance.

   Your turn:

   _____

   _____

   _____

Worksheet: Grounding Using Your 5 Senses

Grounding exercises aim to disconnect you from intense emotions by connecting you to the present. This exercise will ask you to use your five senses: *sight, smell, sound, touch,* and *taste.*

Remember, there are no correct or incorrect answers here. Just provide what's being asked.

List FIVE (5) things you can see right now.

Example: desk plant, hand lotion, water bottle, Nespresso machine, post-it note

1.

2.

3.

4.

5.

List FOUR (4) things you can touch right now.

Example: my sweater, my hair, the chair I'm sitting on, my anti-anxiety bracelet

1.

2.

3.

4.

List THREE (3) things you can hear right now.

Example: my colleague in the next cubicle, people typing on their keyboards, food delivery guy

1.

2.

3.

List TWO (2) things you can smell right now.

Example: hand gel, office room scent

1.

2.

List ONE (1) thing you can taste right now.

Example: coffee

1.

If you're still distressed, repeat the activity or write down as many things as possible.

Worksheet: Self-Soothing Using Your 5 Senses

In the previous exercise, you learned how to use your five senses to *distract* yourself from any intense or unpleasant emotions you might be feeling—as they were happening.

The exercise below is about *planning ahead*. Write at least one thing that offers comfort or is soothing to you for each sense. This way, you know exactly what to do whenever you're in distress in the future. (**Tip**: Aim to self-soothe for at least five (5) minutes whenever you're in distress.)

☐ **Touch**: _____

Example: grab my favorite sweater and wear it like an embrace

☐ **Smell**: _____

Example: go to my terrace garden and smell the roses I planted last summer

☐ **Taste**: _____

Example: pop a peppermint in my mouth

☐ **See**: _____

Example: watch adorable cat videos on YouTube

☐ **Hear**: _____

Example: listen to my favorite DANCE songs

Worksheet: The Happy Place

It can help to mentally leave the situation and imagine yourself in a calming, relaxing, and nurturing place when in distress. Here are the steps to do this:

1. Locate a quiet, comfortable spot where you can sit or lie down without being bothered.
2. Shut your eyes and exhale deeply, releasing any tension in your body.
3. Visualize a peaceful and relaxing place in your head. This could be a beach, a forest, a mountain, or any other peaceful setting. The image might be a real-life location or one that you've entirely invented in your head.
4. Begin by visualizing your environment's colors, forms, and textures. Envision the scene's details as vividly as possible.
5. Try to engage all of your senses as you continue to envision the scene. For example, if you're visualizing a restful day at the beach, imagine the feel of the sun on your skin, the gentle sound of the waves, the smell of the ocean, and the beautiful sunset.
6. While you immerse yourself in the image, pay attention to the sensations in your body. Consider any places of tension or discomfort and envision them dissolving.
7. Let yourself fully absorb the tranquility and calmness of the setting by staying with the visualization for as long as you like.
8. When you're finished, take a few deep breaths and slowly open your eyes. Reflect on the sense of calm and relaxation you just experienced and carry it with you for the remainder of your day.

Worksheet: Into the Cold

When submerged in water, the Mammalian Dive Response (MDR) is a physiological response that occurs in mammals, including humans. It promotes oxygen conservation by slowing the heart rate, redirecting blood flow to the vital organs, and releasing more oxygenated blood into the body.

In humans, the MDR kicks in when the face comes into contact with cold water. It activates our parasympathetic nervous system, the network of nerves that urges the body to slow down and relax.[37] The following exercise teaches you how to activate the MDR when in distress.

CAUTION: Exposing your face to cold water reduces your heart rate. Before performing any of these activities, please check with your doctor if you have a heart condition or are allergic to cold temperatures.

Depression can be triggered anytime, anywhere. For this reason, I encourage you to devise a plan for when you are at home or in public. I've started the table with a few ideas to jumpstart the list. Please add your ideas or what you feel will work best for you.

AT HOME	IN PUBLIC
o Take a VERY COLD shower.	o Go to the restroom and repeatedly wash your face with icy water.
o Open the freezer door and stick your face in it for a while.	o If it's winter, go outside and brave the cold.
o Fill a zip-lock bag with water and place it in the refrigerator. When in distress, grab the bag and place it over your face while holding your breath. (This deceives your brain into believing you're underwater.)	o Buy a water bottle that can keep cold water for hours. When distressed, go to the washroom and pour the cold water all over your face.
o Fill a basin halfway with cold water and immerse your face in it.	o If you can access a refrigerator, store a face gel mask in it and use it as needed.

AT HOME	IN PUBLIC

Other ideas:

Worksheet: STOP

STOP is a DBT activity that can help you gain control of your emotions and avoid acting on them.

S	Stop. Stop! Freeze in place and remain motionless. Don't even twitch a muscle. Physically stopping prevents you from doing what your emotions demand you do. For example, I turned to junk food in my teens to deal with depression. I didn't care about what I ate or drank. Now, I understand the importance of nutrition to mental health. So, whenever I notice symptoms of depression, I freeze whenever I want to reach out for something unhealthy.
T	Take a step back. Take yourself out of the situation. Take a deep breath and hold it for as long as you need to until you regain control. Don't let your emotions dictate your behavior. Remember, we rarely need to make split-second decisions over anything, so take your time before making any decisions.
O	Observe. Mindfully observe what's going on inside and outside of you. Observe as if you were writing a list. (**Note**: You can observe your emotions, i.e., your feelings. However, if this isn't helpful, limit your self-observation to physical aspects.) *An example of self-observation:* *I have a terrible migraine, and my head is pounding.*

What are you observing about yourself?

_____

_____

_____

An example of observing your environment:
My desk plant looks dry, and my water bottle is empty. I smell coffee.

What are you observing about your environment?

_____

_____

_____

P Proceed mindfully.

Okay, you've taken a break from the distressful situation, and now it's time to move forward—with caution. Ask yourself, "*How can I improve this situation?*" or "*What can I do to feel better?*" Be as detailed as you can with how you want to proceed.

Example:
I have a terrible migraine, and my head is pounding.
I'm going to (1) get up, (2) count my steps as I walk to the bathroom, (3) wash my face with very cold water, (4) open the medicine cabinet, (5) reach for and take paracetamol, (6) and lie down for a few minutes.

What do you want to do to proceed mindfully?

_____

_____

_____

TIPP skills help you tolerate your distress by changing your body's chemistry. Research shows that by altering your *physical* state, you also positively alter your mental and emotional states.[38,39]

T	**T**emperature. Our body temperature rises in stressful conditions. Cool your body down to counteract this physical stress response. (**Tip**: See Into the Cold, page 83.)
I	**I**ntense Exercise. During stressful situations, you may have a lot of pent-up energy. However, instead of reacting to intense emotions negatively, such as self-harming behaviors or unhealthy eating, it's better to channel that energy into something positive, such as engaging in intense physical activities (e.g., jumping jacks, running, HIIT sessions, etc.). Also, research shows that exercising is a great mood enhancer[40], so you'll feel much better after engaging in intense physical activities. When you're depressed, you might find intense exercise a difficult choice if *low energy* is one of your depressive symptoms. But remember that exercising boosts energy levels[41], so even if you don't feel like it, you'll help your disorder by exercising anyway. Here are a few tips to motivate you to move, despite what your depression is telling you.

1. **Make exercising an EASY choice.** If we perceive exercising as difficult, we might not do it despite our best intentions. So make exercising an easy choice by removing potential obstacles.

   For example, if you want to join a gym, choose one close to your home or workplace so it's easy to get there. If you prefer to workout in the mornings, lay your exercise clothes beside your bed the night before.

2. **Start with small goals.** Instead of trying to jump into an entire workout routine, start with small and achievable goals. For example, walk around the block quickly or go up and down a flight of stairs until you run out of breath.

3. **Devise a plan—or not.** Some people work best with a routine. If you're such a person, set a specific time and place for exercise. Write it down in your calendar or planner. Having a plan can help you stay accountable and motivated.

   On the other hand, if being spontaneous is more you, that's okay too. Fit in exercise whenever and wherever you can.

4. **Find a workout buddy.** Exercising with a friend or family member can make it more enjoyable and help keep you motivated. You can also hold each other accountable and provide support when needed.

5. **Choose an enjoyable activity.** Pick an activity you enjoy, whether dancing, swimming, running, or playing a sport. You're likelier to stick with the activity and find it less of a chore when

you enjoy it.

6. **Focus on the benefits.** Remind yourself of the benefits of exercise, such as improved mood and energy, reduced stress, and better sleep. Focusing on these positive outcomes can help motivate you to get moving.

7. **Just do it.** Adopt a 'no excuses' attitude when it comes to exercising. For example, if you find exercising hard during the day, purchase low-cost exercise equipment that you can use at home. For example, resistance bands can help you do a quick 5–10 minute strength-training routine at home. Can't leave your office? Buy a cheap under-desk bike (also called a "desk cycle") to get some exercise while you work.

   You can also use apps like _5 Minute Home Workouts_ by Olson Applications, _7 Minute Workout_ by Workout Apps, _FitOn Workouts_ by FitOn, and others to get in some fast exercise throughout the day.

Paced Breathing.

P Intense emotions tend to increase our breathing. Slow it down by deliberately and mindfully controlling your breath. (**Tip**: Do any or all of the Mindfulness breathing exercises.)

Paired Muscle Relaxation.

P Paced Breathing can be combined with Paired Muscle Relaxation. While you take a deep breath, steadily tighten your muscles, but not so much that they cramp. When you exhale, slowly relax your tensed-up muscles.

Tip: When you're right in the middle of a crisis, do Paced Breathing + Paired Muscle Relaxation for a few minutes. (See also Body Scan Muscle Relaxation on the next page.)

Worksheet: Body Scan Muscle Relaxation

This exercise systematically combines Paced Breathing and Muscle Relaxation, promoting mental and emotional relaxation and reducing physical tension.

1. Find a quiet and comfortable place to lie on your back or sit in a chair with your feet flat.
2. Close your eyes and take a few deep breaths to relax and calm your mind.
3. Bring your attention to your body and observe any tension or discomfort.
4. **Begin at your toes.** Start the body scan at your toes, and focus on them. Tighten the muscles in your toes and hold for a few seconds, then release and relax them completely.
5. **Move up to your feet and ankles.** Move your attention up to your feet and ankles. Tighten the muscles in your feet and ankles and hold for a few seconds, then release and relax them completely.
6. **Progress to your calves and thighs.** Continue moving your attention up your body to your calves and thighs. Tighten the muscles in your calves and thighs and hold for a few seconds, then release and relax them completely.
7. **Focus on your stomach and chest**. Move your attention up to your stomach and chest. Tighten the muscles in your stomach and chest and hold for a few seconds, then release and relax them completely.
8. **Move up to your shoulders and arms.** Continue up to your shoulders and arms. Tighten the muscles in your shoulders and arms and hold for a few seconds, then release and relax them completely.
9. **End at your face and head**. Finish the body scan at your face and head. Tighten the muscles in your face and hold for a few seconds, then release and relax them completely.
10. Take a few deep breaths and notice how relaxed your whole body feels.
11. Stay relaxed for a few minutes, enjoying the feeling of relaxation throughout your body.

Worksheet: ACCEPTS

When you're depressed, what do you want to do? What's the emotional urge or impulse you have? For me, it was to self-isolate and turn to junk food. For others, it's to engage in negative self-talk (e.g., *I'm worthless, I'm ugly, I'm fat,* etc.). For others still, it's to take "depression naps" and stay in bed for hours.

One of the things I realized in my mental health journey is that my emotional urges or impulses exacerbated my mental health problems. **ACCEPTS** is a DBT exercise that has helped me NOT ACT on my emotional urges, and I hope it does the same for you.

A

Activities.

Create a list of activities you enjoy. Preferably, list down activities that require your undivided attention. The goal is to thoroughly immerse yourself in the activity and be "in the zone." Also, consider activities that will mentally or physically stimulate you. For instance, reading a self-help book is preferable to mindlessly scrolling through social networking sites.

Examples: paint, binge-watch your all-time favorite program on Netflix, swim laps, etc.

List down as many attention-grabbing activities as you like below.

1. _____
2. _____
3. _____
4. _____
5. _____
6. _____
7. _____
8. _____

9. _____

10. _____

Contribute.

When we're depressed, we may become self-absorbed (e.g., *Why is this happening to me?, What did I do to deserve this? Why am I like this?* etc.)

So, instead of focusing on yourself, *focus on others*. According to studies, thinking about others' needs benefits not only the people you help but also benefits you psychologically and physically, making you healthier and extending your life span.[42]

Examples: cook a meal for someone, go through your pantry or kitchen cupboards and gather canned goods to donate, do volunteer work

C

What do you want to contribute? List as many ideas as you can.

1. _____

2. _____

3. _____

4. _____

5. _____

6. _____

7. _____

8. _____

9. _____

10. _____

Compare.

Another way to divert your attention away from your *current situation* is to compare it to past experiences. The goal here is to realize that you're stronger than you think. You survived a previous depressive episode, so you will this time too!

Example:
Two months ago, I neglected my personal hygiene. I think I only washed my hair once that month. I survived that depressive episode, and I will survive this one too.

To which past even do you want to make a comparison?

_____

_____

_____

Emotions.

Distract yourself from persistent sadness and despair by doing something that will illicit the opposite emotion (i.e., joy or happiness).

Examples: make a gratitude list, walk in nature, go to the mirror and smile at yourself again and again, do Loving Kindness Meditation *(page 67)*

_____

_____

_____

P

Push away.

PUSH AWAY whatever impulse comes to mind when you're depressed. For example, you might want to discontinue your sessions if you're undergoing therapy. You might think, *"I'm in therapy, but I'm still depressed. It isn't working. I think I should stop."*

If you give in to such impulses, you might do yourself more harm than good. So, instead of entertaining such thoughts, push them away.

Here are some suggestions for "pushing away." Feel free to add your thoughts as well.

- ☐ Go to a quiet place where you can be alone, then yell, "STOP!"
- ☐ Do The Silver Lining exercise (page 45).
- ☐ Try a visual imagery exercise like The Happy Place, page 82.
- ☐ Others:_____

_____

_____

_____

T

Thoughts.

Distract yourself with "other" thoughts.

Examples:

If you're thinking of crying, sing a happy song in your head.

If you're having dinner at your parent's place, and something is depressing you, start counting the colors you can see in the room.

Your turn:

_____

_____

_____

S

Sensations.

Distract yourself by exposing your body to different physical sensations.
Here are some examples. Feel free to add your thoughts as well.

- ☐ Drink an overly sweet drink.
- ☐ Chew a sourball.
- ☐ Put some pepper flakes in your mouth.
- ☐ Chew ginger candy.
- ☐ Take a VERY COLD shower.
- ☐ Others:

_____

_____

_____

Worksheet: IMPROVE

IMPROVE skills teach you how to make distressing or depressing moments better.

I	**I**magery. Mentally visualize yourself in a better place. *Examples:* *Imagine all your aches, pains, and sadness washing away from you like soap suds while showering.* *Remember a time in your life when you were truly happy and bring yourself back to that moment by trying to remember every detail about it.* Your turn: _____ _____ _____
M	**M**eaning. Try to find meaning in your emotional suffering. (See also <u>The Silver Lining</u>, page 45). *Examples:* *This sadness will make it easier to appreciate future moments of joy and happiness.* Flist at

Your turn:

_____
_____
_____

P

Prayer.

Turn to a greater power for strength and comfort. Research shows that praying boosts mental health by offering emotional comfort and decreasing mental health disorder symptoms.[43,44] (Note: If you're not religious, consider asking advice from someone you respect.)

Example:
Say this out loud: "Please give me the strength I need to bear this."

Your turn:

_____
_____
_____

R

Relaxation.

Engage in calming activities that might help you relax and clear your mind. List down at least three (3) calming activities.

Examples: walking with my dog in the woods, cooking, watching my favorite feel-good movies

1 _____

2 _____

3 _____

One thing at a time.

Focus on one specific activity. Don't think about anything other than what you're doing right now.

Example: I'm touching my calming bracelet. My eyes are closed, and I'm letting the smoothness of the calming beads relax me. I'm also tuning my breath with how I touch the beads. I inhale as I rub one bead and exhale as I go on to the next.

What are you doing?

_____

_____

Describe this moment in as many details as you can.

_____

_____

_____

Vacation.

Give yourself a break from adulthood and take a vacation. However, please note that these vacations should only be brief, and you shouldn't use them as your primary way of dealing with depression. Doing so may lead to *avoidance coping*, a negative way to deal with mental health problems.

Example:
Take the afternoon off. Go to a nearby café and get drinks, a sandwich, or a nice pastry treat. Next, visit a nearby park and treat yourself to an afternoon picnic.

Your turn:

_____

_____

_____

Encouragement.

Be your own cheerleader! This may be harder than you think because we're often our worst critics. Also, people suffering from depression may feel guilt and loathing for themselves. As such, practice this skill by imagining yourself offering advice to your best friend.

Example: Hey, you're doing the best you can. You've survived depression before, and you can do it again. You may not see it now, but it will be okay.

Your turn:

_____

_____

_____

E

Worksheet: Radical Acceptance When Feeling Depressed

As previously discussed, Radical Acceptance (page 46) is accepting the reality of your present situation. You accept you're suffering from depression because you want to be free of the emotional suffering it brings. You want to focus on feeling and being better.

The following worksheet will help you learn how to apply Radical Acceptance during a depressive episode.

1. **OBSERVE.** Notice how you might be fighting reality or questioning it.

   List down how you're ignoring, fighting, or rejecting your depression.
   Example: Thinking or saying, "No, no, no. This cannot be happening again!"

   _____

   _____

   _____

2. **REMEMBER.** Remind yourself that the existing situation (reality) is something that you cannot change.

   Write down your own depression acceptance statement.
   Example: I'm depressed. I don't like it, but it is what it is.

   _____

   _____

   _____

3. **RATIONALIZE.** Tell yourself that this current situation is not without reason. That is, "NOW" didn't happen by chance, and there are reasons why things transpired the way they did.

This is how I rationalized my depression (i.e., this is how things happened): *I'm depressed now, not "just because" but because of many things in my past, such as the chaos, lack of security, and emotional instability I experienced at home. This was followed by the alienation and extreme loneliness I felt during my adolescence and the development of my OCD and anxiety disorders.*

How did things happen?

_____

_____

_____

_____

_____

4. **ACCEPT.** Practice acceptance of the situation with your whole being. That is, not just mentally but emotionally and physically as well.

Accept with your mind:
Example: Say, "This is the situation, and it is what it is."

_____

_____

Accept with your heart:
Example: Say, "I'm a good person; depression doesn't change this."

_____

_____

Accept with your body:

Example: Suppose you're sitting with your head bowed and between your hands. In this case, slowly and deliberately release your head, then sit or stand up straight.

_____

_____

5. **OPPOSITE ACTION.** Do the exact opposite of what your depression dictates you do.

Example:
I don't want to take a shower. So I will get up, head straight to the bathroom and take one.

Your turn:

_____

_____

_____

6. **IMAGINE ACCEPTANCE.** If you're still having trouble accepting your situation, try imagining how it would be to accept it. Paint a picture in your head of the possible positive consequences of accepting.

Examples:
If I accept, I can move on, think, and do something else.

Your turn:

_____

_____

_____

_____

7. **ATTEND.** Pay attention to your physical reactions while considering what you need to accept. If you notice any physical resistance to your situation (e.g., folding your arms across your chest, frowning, clenching your teeth, etc.), address it.

   Example: While visualizing acceptance, I can feel myself starting to clench my fists. I should do some deep breathing and open my hands wide each time I exhale.

   Your turn:

   _____

   _____

   _____

   _____

   _____

8. **ALLOW AND THEN LET GO.** Give yourself permission to feel grief, loneliness, or sadness. Remember that acceptance is not approval or being okay with the situation. So, there's no need to deny your emotions. Let them come... and then let them go.

   Example:
   I'm so sad and lonely and don't have anyone to talk to or share anything with. And then imagine letting these emotions go like water sliding off you.

   Your turn:

   _____

   _____

   _____

9. **ACKNOWLEDGE.** Recognize that even when things are hard, life is still worth living.

Example:
I'm not always this way; I have known happiness before. So, I will cling to the hope that I can be happy again.

Your turn:

_____

_____

_____

"Emotional self-regulation is not the suppression of emotions, but the regulation of their intensity and expression."
— *John Gottman*

Emotions are reactions. They can be positive, such as happiness, love, and excitement, or negative, such as sadness, anger, and fear. Emotions are our responses to external or internal stimuli. For example, seeing a beautiful sunset may trigger feelings of contentment or happiness. In contrast, internal thoughts, like worrying about a looming deadline, may trigger feelings of anxiousness or fear.

Emotions are important to our identity because they significantly affect our daily lives. You may not notice it, but your emotions greatly dictate your actions. If you engage in an activity that makes you happy, you will most likely keep on doing that activity. If someone makes you angry, then you might reciprocate with anger or avoid that person.

It's important to remember that feeling an emotion doesn't cause problems. How you understand or interpret emotions is what determines whether the stimuli (internal or external) will become a problem or not.

As previously mentioned, depression is a mood disorder characterized by *persistent* feelings of sadness and despair. As such, people with depression are in a vicious cycle of negative emotions.

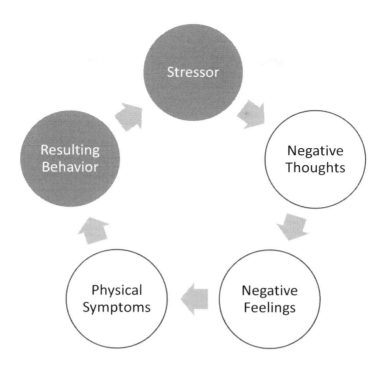

For me, the above cycle would look something like this:

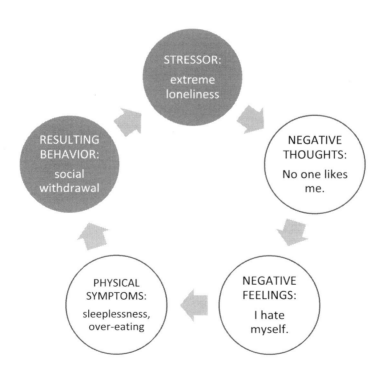

Speaking from experience, I know that breaking this cycle is hard. However, if we don't try, then the vicious cycle of depression continues, and we prolong our own suffering.

Emotion Regulation is about breaking the cycle of negative emotions, thoughts, and behavior. It's about controlling and managing your emotions instead of letting them control you.

On the following pages are various exercises that will help you decrease your emotional reactivity to your depression and increase your ability to experience and tolerate a wide range of emotions.

Worksheet: Understanding and Labeling Your Emotions

Often, our emotions are difficult to manage because we don't fully understand them. Several years ago, I was asked how depression feels and replied, *"It's like a big ball of sadness."* When asked to explain further, I felt speechless and realized I didn't know how to dig deep and describe my emotions.

If you're experiencing the same, then please do the following exercise. The more you can properly define your depression, the easier it will be to regulate the emotions contributing to it. This, in turn, will help you make more intentional choices about how to respond to your depressive stressors.

1. **Mindfulness**. Take a few minutes to sit quietly and tune in to your emotions.

2. **Specifics**. Try to label your emotions as precisely as possible. For example, see if you can narrow your sadness to any of the following:

   - ☐ disappointment
   - ☐ grief
   - ☐ loneliness
   - ☐ embarrassment
   - ☐ emptiness
   - ☐ abandonment
   - ☐ Others:

   _____
   _____
   _____

3. **Intensity levels.** Consider the intensity of the emotion you're feeling. Is it a mild emotion, like a mood, or more intense, like extreme sadness? Encircle the intensity level of your feelings below, with 1 being the least intense and 10 being the most.

| 1 | 2 | 3 | 4 | 5 | 6 | 7 | 8 | 9 | 10 |

4. **Reason.** Do your best to identify what might be causing your emotion. Is it related to a recent event, a particular thought or memory, or an ongoing situation in your life? Write down your thoughts about the situation that applies to you. (You don't need to fill out all the items below; just the one(s) directly related to the emotion you're feeling now.)

☐ Recent event / Something that recently happened:
Example: A friend canceled our dinner plans at the last minute. I feel disappointed and alone.

_____

_____

_____

☐ Thought/memory:
Example: My mom passed away a year ago, and today I saw sunflowers, her favorite flower.

_____

_____

_____

☐ Someone I know
Example: A co-worker took credit for work I've done. I'm mad and sad.

_____

_____

_____

☐ Ongoing situation:

Example: I don't have friends.

_____

_____

_____

5. **Reflect**. Finally, take a few moments to reflect on how your emotion affects you.

    ☐ Any negative thoughts?

Example: I don't have friends... it's making me think I'm just not a likable person.

_____

_____

_____

    ☐ Any negative feelings?

Example: I don't have friends... I feel horrible and worthless.

_____

_____

_____

    ☐ Any physical symptoms?

Example: I don't have friends... I'm so anxious about it. I have migraines all the time.

_____

_____

_____

☐ Any emotional impulses or urges?

Example: I don't have friends... all I want to do is stay in bed all day.

_____

_____

_____

At the end of this exercise, you should understand what's causing your depression, how you're feeling about it, and how you're reacting to it.

Worksheet: The Wave

After <u>Understanding and Labeling Your Emotions</u> in the previous exercise, you'll learn how to let go of painful emotions.

Remember that letting go does not mean denying or rejecting your emotions. However, when we're sad and depressed, we may become stuck when we try to process negative emotions. Instead of just letting them go, we might hold on to them even tighter, thinking about every detail of how we feel and wondering why it's happening to us.

So after understanding and labeling your emotions, accept them, and then let them go. Here are the steps on how to do this:

1. **Radically accept.** Acknowledge your feelings with your heart, body, and mind by stating acceptance statements.

   Example: I felt lonely and depressed when my friend canceled our dinner plans. I was looking forward to it, and their decision to cancel made it seem like they didn't care. Still, the dinner is canceled, and I can't do anything about it now. It is what it is.

   _____

   _____

   _____

   _____

   _____

   _____

2. **The Wave.** Next, try to experience your feelings as a wave that's coming and going. However, imagine the waves getting weaker and weaker. For example, close your eyes and imagine "loneliness" as a wave approaching you. Don't be afraid or try to avoid it. Let it come. Let it touch you. Let it wash away.

Next, imagine "loneliness" as a wave coming at you again, but this time, the wave is smaller and gentler. Just like before, let it reach you and let it wash away.

Practice The Wave for each and every unpleasant emotion you might be feeling. If it helps, combine The Wave with any breathing exercise under <u>Mindfulness</u> (page 55).

Worksheet: Check the Facts

When we're depressed, it's difficult to step back and think about whether our feelings are in line with what happened. **Check the Facts** is a way to stop, think, and examine if our emotions match the facts.

Let's start with a reflective exercise. Think back to a previous situation when you may have acted too quickly in response to your emotions.

Question: What emotion do you want to fact-check?
Example: my feelings of abandonment
Your answer:

Question: What happened? What triggered this emotion?
Example: My friend canceled our dinner plans last-minute.
Your answer:

Question: What assumptions did you make about the event?
Example: They didn't care about me at all. I'm unimportant, so it's easy for them to cancel on me.
Your answer:

Question: What did you do?

Example: I got depressed. I didn't go to work for a few days and didn't answer their calls or text messages.

Your answer:

CHECK THE FACTS!

You listed your assumptions above, but <u>WHAT ELSE</u> could the situation mean? Try to think of the situation as a whole, not just from your point of view.

Question: What do you know FOR SURE?

Example: My friend canceled our dinner plans last minute.

Your answer:

Question: Are your assumptions about the event supported by FACTS?

What's your assumption?

Example assumption: My friend doesn't care about me at all. I'm unimportant, so it's easy for them to cancel on me.

Is this supported by FACTS?

Example: No. Now that I think about it, they said sorry about canceling last minute and will tell me the reason for canceling in person.

Question: Why do you think you reacted that way?

Example: My feelings of low self-esteem kicked in. I couldn't stop feeling abandoned.

Your answer:

Question: Looking back, on a scale of 0-5, did your emotion fit the facts? (0 = not at all, 5 = yes):

Example: 0

Your answer:

Question: If your emotion DID NOT fit the facts, what would you do differently?

Example: First, I would do Distress Tolerance exercises (page 74) to ease my pain. Then I'd do Check the Facts to put my emotions into perspective. Lastly, I would've gone to work and answered their calls and text messages.

Your answer:

Question: If your emotion DID fit the facts, would you do anything differently?

Example: Yes. Instead of staying home, which just prolonged my depressive episode, I should've found other, more positive ways of dealing with my emotions.

Your answer:

Note: You can use **Check the Facts** whenever you feel unpleasant emotions. It's not just a reflective exercise. Still, I recommend repeating this exercise at least twice more to develop the habit of fact-checking your emotions.

Worksheet: Opposite Action

One of the best ways to avoid acting on negative impulses or urges is to train yourself to do the opposite of what your emotions are telling you.

For example, if I could go back to my adolescent self, I would NOT socially withdraw and self-isolate because those actions only made my depression worse. Instead, I would tell my younger self to build on my self-esteem, be brave, and attempt to make friends. I've always received good marks, so I could have volunteered to tutor younger children to boost my self-esteem. I also attended a multicultural school. If I had only tried harder, I might have found other immigrant students with whom I shared more interests. But I didn't do any of those things. Instead, I gave in to what my emotions demanded.

Opposite Action is an excellent exercise to prevent you from acting on emotional impulses. It requires some pre-planning, so please take your time in accomplishing the table below.

Column A lists down unpleasant emotions. **Column B** is where you write what you usually do when experiencing these emotions. Lastly, **Column C** is where you should write down your counter-action.

Whenever you're depressed and feel the need to "act out" Column B, refer to this table and do what you wrote under Column C instead. I've filled out some of the rows to jumpstart ideas. Please feel free to add your own.

OPPOSITE ACTION

A	B	C
Emotion	**Emotional Impulse**	**Opposite Action**
What you are feeling.	*What do you usually do when you feel this way?*	*Write down your opposite action here.*
Emptiness	Eat cake and ice cream to feel better	Exercise
Sadness	Cry, avoid people	Seek contact
Inferior	Negative self-talk	Practice Loving Kindness Meditation (page 67)
Loneliness	Hide, self-harm	
Fear	Stay indoors	
Hurt	Self-blame, internalize	
Vulnerable	Say "Yes" to everyone even if I don't want to	

OPPOSITE ACTION

A	B	C
Emotion	**Emotional Impulse**	**Opposite Action**
What you are feeling.	*What do you usually do when you feel this way?*	*Write down your opposite action here.*
Feel free to add more emotions and scenarios in the extra rows below.		

Worksheet: Build Positive Experiences (BPE)

Build your resilience to depression by increasing positive feelings in your life. Imagine having an "emotional cup." If you fill it with as many positive emotions as possible, there's only so much room left for negative ones, right?

Build **P**ositive **E**xperiences (BPE) teaches you how to accumulate more positive, happy moments in your life.

Build Positive Experiences I

Make a list of 10 experiences that make you happy. These positive experiences should make you feel good while performing them or shortly after.

Examples: walking in nature, doing Pilates, journaling, etc.

1.

2.

3.

4.

5.

6.

7.

8.

9.

10.

Build Positive Experiences II

Pick ONE activity from the list above and commit to doing it every day. It makes no difference what you decide to do or how long you want to do it. The objective is to do the activity EVERY SINGLE DAY. (Make happiness a daily habit!)

Example: walking in nature
I will <u>take a walk</u> every day for <u>30 minutes in the morning</u>.

Your turn:

I choose: _____

I will _____ every day for _____.

Build Positive Experiences III

Make a list of 10 experiences that have the potential to provide you long-term enjoyment. You may need to plan these activities, but when they occur, they have a long-term positive impact on your life.

Examples: traveling to Europe, getting a puppy, etc.

1.

2.

3.

4.

5.

6.

7.

8.

9.

10.

Worksheet: Accumulate, Build, Cope (ABC)

ABC is similar to BPE in that the goal is to increase your resilience to depression by increasing moments of positivity and happiness. The difference is the addition of the **C** skill (Cope Ahead), which aims to prepare you for situations that may trigger a depressive episode.

A

Accumulate Positive Emotions.

Short-Term Positive Emotions

Create a list of **10 positive activities** you can do today to bring you joy.

Examples: 10-minute mental break, yoga, dancing, etc.

1. _____
2. _____
3. _____
4. _____
5. _____
6. _____
7. _____
8. _____
9. _____
10. _____

Long-Term Positive Emotions

Create a list of **10 positive changes** you want to make so that positive events happen more frequently in the future.

Examples: stop eating junk food TO improve my health, build my self-confidence TO make new friends

1. _____ *to* _____
2. _____ *to* _____
3. _____ *to* _____
4. _____ *to* _____
5. _____ *to* _____
6. _____ *to* _____
7. _____ *to* _____
8. _____ *to* _____
9. _____ *to* _____
10. _____ *to* _____

Build Mastery.

Excelling at something builds self-esteem and fights feelings of helplessness, sadness, and despair. List at least five things you want to learn or something you already do well but want to be better at.

Examples: baking, painting, HTML coding, etc.

B

1. _____
2. _____
3. _____
4. _____
5. _____

Cope Ahead.

Is there a specific situation or person that triggers your depression? If so, planning how to cope when encountering that situation or person would be beneficial.

Whatever plan you devise, rehearse it in your mind or roleplay it with someone. Practicing what you will say and do during the situation will help you cope with it better.

Question: What's the stressful event that usually triggers your depression?

Example: Sunday family gatherings

_____

_____

_____

Question: What usually happens? What are you concerned about?

Example: The chaos stresses me out. Somehow, my parents end up fighting, my sister always sides with my mom, and I'm left to side with my dad. At the end of the meal, everyone's upset. When I leave, I feel guilty, sad, and depressed for the coming days.

_____

_____

_____

_____

_____

_____

Cope Ahead Plan

1. Rehearse the situation in your mind.
2. Plan what you plan to DO. Be as detailed as possible.

Example:

- *When the fighting starts, I will do <u>Equal Breathing</u> (page 61).*
- *When my parents start to make digs at each other, I'll do <u>Happy Place</u> (page 82).*
- *When my father asks me to side with him (again), I'll say, "Sorry, Dad, this is between you and mom." If my dad persists, I'll say, "Sorry, Dad, this is between you and mom." I will say this over and over and over until my dad leaves me alone.*
- *If I start feeling guilty, I'll say to myself, "This is not on me. This is not on me. This is not on me."*
- *When I get home, I won't even give my depression a chance. I'll do any of the activities I listed under <u>Build Positive Experiences (BPE)</u>, page 122.*

Your turn:

_____

_____

_____

_____

_____

_____

_____

_____

_____

_____

_____

Important: When you practice your Cope Ahead plan, it's normal to experience negative emotions because you're reliving the potential stressor as if it were happening. So, it's imperative to take a break and chill out afterward.

Make a list of things that calm you.

Examples: a cup of calming tea, journaling, hugging my dog, etc.

1. _____

2. _____

3. _____

4. _____

5. _____

6. _____

7. _____

8. _____

9. _____

10. _____

Worksheet: PLEASE

Your physical health is directly related to your emotional health and vice versa.[45] An unhealthy body makes you more vulnerable to negative emotions. In contrast, taking care of your body improves your emotional resiliency.

PL	## Treat **P**hysical i**ll**ness without delay. You must protect your health because illness lowers your resistance to negative emotions. As such, if you're feeling physically ill, don't put off seeing a doctor or taking any prescribed medications. It's also advisable to contact someone (e.g., a family member, friend, neighbor, colleague, etc.) to be with you so that you're not alone while you're sick. If you don't want to see a doctor or are physically unable to, consider a holistic approach to treatment, such as acupuncture, aromatherapy, acupressure, yoga, etc. The goal is to get well as soon as possible. When was the last time you were physically ill? _____ Did you see a doctor? Y / N Why or why not? _____ _____ _____
E	## Balanced **E**ating. We are what we eat.[46] This means the foods we consume affect our overall health and well-being, so nourishing our bodies with food that affects us positively is essential. For example, a diet high in processed

foods and sugar may contribute to feelings of anxiety and depression[47]. In contrast, a diet rich in whole foods and healthy fats may help improve mood and cognitive function[48].

So, as much as possible, eat food as close to its natural state. For example, instead of buying and consuming a jar of peanut butter, invest in a kitchen processor, buy whole peanuts, and make your own peanut butter. Plenty of websites share how to make your favorite foods from scratch, so just put Google to good use.

Important: Before making any significant changes to your diet, you should always talk to your doctor or a nutritionist. (See also <u>Nutrition: Eat to Beat Depression</u>, page 154.)

<u>A</u>void Unhealthy Substances.

Unhealthy substances such as alcohol and illegal drugs can make depression worse.[49] Instead, drink plain water, lemon water, green tea, healthy smoothies, etc.

What about coffee? Caffeine is a stimulant that can boost alertness and improve mood in some people. However, excessive caffeine consumption can contribute to anxiety and depression.[50] Generally, an 8-ounce (240 ml) cup of coffee has about 100 mg of caffeine. Several sites say that most healthy adults can have 400 mg of caffeine daily, the same as 4 cups (945 ml) of coffee. [51,52] As such, it's best to monitor your own reaction to coffee.

<u>S</u>leep.

The American Academy of Sleep Medicine (AAS) and the Sleep Research Society (SRS) both say that adults need at least seven (7) hours of quality sleep every night.[53] Quality sleep is restful and uninterrupted, allowing one to wake up feeling refreshed and energized.

Unfortunately, sleep problems are common symptoms of depression. *Insomnia* occurs when you are unable to fall asleep or have difficulty staying asleep, or when you wake up too early and are unable to return to sleep. *Hypersomnia* occurs when you experience excessive daytime sleepiness and have difficulty staying awake during the day. If you suffer from any of these symptoms, here are some tips to help you.

1. Maintain a **consistent sleeping routine**. Even on weekends, go to bed and wake up at the same time every day.
2. Create a **relaxing sleep environment**. Ensure your bedroom is cool, dark, and quiet, and avoid screens before bedtime.
3. **Limit caffeine, alcohol, and nicotine.** These substances can interfere with sleep quality, so avoiding them in the evening or before bed is best.
4. Get **regular exercise**. Regular physical activity can help promote better sleep but avoid vigorous exercise close to bedtime.
5. **Avoid large meals and fluids before bedtime**. Eating a big meal or drinking a lot of fluids before bedtime can disrupt sleep.
6. **Wind down before bed.** Do relaxing activities before bedtime, such as taking a warm bath or reading a book.
7. **Manage stress.** Stress and anxiety can make it hard to fall asleep, so it's important to find ways to deal with stress throughout the day.
8. Use **comfortable bedding**. Purchase a comfortable mattress and

pillows that support good sleep posture.

9. **Avoid napping** during the day. If you have trouble sleeping at night, avoid napping during the day.

10. Seek **professional help** if needed. If you still have difficulties sleeping despite making lifestyle changes, consult a doctor to rule out any underlying medical issues or sleep disorders like sleep apnea or narcolepsy.

E

Exercise.

Research has shown that exercising can make you feel happier and less sad.[54,55] One reason for this is that it can increase the release of *endorphins* in the brain. Endorphins are neurotransmitters that act as natural painkillers and mood elevators. This release of endorphins can lead to feelings of euphoria and well-being, often referred to as a "runner's high."

According to the World Health Organization, adults 18-64 should do at least 2.5 to 5 hours of moderate-intensity aerobic physical activity or 1.25 to 2.5 hours of intense aerobic physical activity weekly. This should ideally be done with muscle-strengthening activities that are moderate to highly intense 2x or more per week.

Important: **PLEASE** skills are not meant to be one-time activities. You should strive to make these activities part of your lifestyle to reap their benefits.

*"The way we communicate with others and with ourselves
ultimately determines the quality of our lives."*
— Tony Robbins

Human beings are social creatures. It's in our nature to want to share our lives with others. As such, relationships are an integral part of human existence. And not only do we want people in our lives, but we also want to be a part of other people's lives.

Relationships make life fulfilling and meaningful. They give us a sense of belonging, provide emotional support, and contribute to our personal growth.

Great communication skills are at the heart of great relationships. Effective communication builds stronger relationships, resolves conflicts, and conveys ideas and information effectively. Bad communication, on the other hand, can lead to misunderstandings, misinterpretations, frustrations, and even the breakdown of relationships.

What is communication?

Communication is when two or more people or groups exchange information, ideas, or feelings. Communication can happen in a number of ways, such as:

1. **Verbal communication** includes spoken language, such as talking or giving a speech.
2. **Nonverbal communication** includes communication without words, such as facial expressions, body language, and tone of voice.
3. **Written communication** includes written forms of communication, such as emails, letters, and texts.

4. **Visual communication** includes communication through visual elements, such as pictures, graphs, and charts.

5. **Gestural communication** includes communication through gestures, such as waving hello or pointing.

6. **Electronic communication** includes communication through electronic devices, such as social media, video chats, and instant messaging.

7. **Touch communication** includes communication through touch, such as a handshake or a hug.

Each form of communication can be effective in different situations and with different people. Effective communication often involves using a combination of these different forms of communication to convey your message clearly and effectively.

However, as mentioned, communication is exchanging information, ideas, or feelings. It's a two-way process.

So, knowing how to communicate YOUR message effectively is just half of the equation. The other half is paying attention and understanding (correctly interpreting) the other party's message.

Researchers have found that people with depression have trouble communicating with other people.[56,57] For example, they often struggle to express themselves clearly, find the right words to describe their thoughts and feelings and speak in a monotone or flat tone. People with depression tend to be more self-critical or negative in their self-talk, making it difficult to express positive emotions and thoughts.

Nonverbal communication problems in people who suffer from depression may include a lack of eye contact, a lack of facial expression, and slumped or closed body posture. These nonverbal cues can affect how others perceive and respond to the person with depression, which can negatively impact communication and social interactions.

Note: Not everyone with depression will experience communication problems. And if they do, the severity and type of communication problems can vary from person to person. Further, communication problems are NOT exclusive to depression and often present in other mental health conditions.

In DBT, **Interpersonal Effectiveness** is about learning how to communicate effectively to get what you want and need from others in a conversation. Additionally, since communication is a two-way process, you'll learn how to build stronger relationships by actively listening to others. You'll also learn about self-respect effectiveness. Research shows that people who suffer from depression tend to be people-pleasers.[58] If you constantly put other people's wants and needs above your own, like by always saying "Yes," you'll lose your self-respect in the long run. On the other hand, you shouldn't betray your values and beliefs (e.g., manipulating, telling lies, etc.) to get what you want or to get people to like you.

Worksheet: Active Listening

Active Listening is about fully focusing on and understanding what the speaker is saying. This way, you'll be able to receive and accurately interpret other people during the communication process, preventing misunderstandings and conflict in the relationship.

Note: When you do this exercise for the first time, pick a neutral or noncontroversial topic (e.g., favorite Netflix TV series, a favorite song, etc.). The goal is to fully understand what the other person is saying, not to get into an argument.

1. **Choose a speaker.** Find someone you can talk with, such as a friend, family member, or coworker.

    Who's your speaker?
    Example: my mom

    _____

2. **Find a quiet time and place.** To minimize distractions, choose a quiet time and location where you can focus on the conversation.

    When and where are you going to have this conversation?
    Example: in the kitchen, when everybody else has left, and it's just my mom and me

    _____

3. **Face the speaker.** Face the person speaking, and maintain eye contact to show you're engaged and interested.

4. **Listen without interruption.** Allow the speaker to completely finish their thoughts before responding. Avoid interrupting, interjecting, or finishing their sentences.

5. **Show interest**. Show that you are interested in what the speaker is saying by nodding, smiling, or using verbal cues such as "*I see,*" "*Okay,*" or "*Uh-huh.*"

6. **Rephrase what you heard**. After the speaker has finished talking, rephrase what you heard to ensure you understood correctly. For example, say, "*Let me make sure I understand. You said...*"

7. **Clarify.** If you're unsure of something the speaker said, ask for clarification. For example, say, "*I don't get it. Why do you...?*"

8. **Provide feedback.** Offer feedback and ask questions to show that you have been actively listening. For example, you say, "*It sounds like you're feeling nostalgic about that song. Am I right?*"

9. **Summarize.** At the end of the conversation, summarize what was discussed to ensure that you understand the topic clearly.

Worksheet: DEARMAN

DEARMAN is about *objective effectiveness*. It's how to effectively and clearly express your needs and desires and get what you want from an interaction. You see, there's an "art" to asking. If you demand, you probably won't get what you want and may even damage your relationships. **DEARMAN** will help you ask effectively.

D	**D**escribe the situation. What do you want or need? Talk about the situation using words that are clear and to the point. Don't say what you think or feel; say what you know to be true. What's the situation? *Example: I want to ask my partner to have more patience with me. I suffer from hypersomnia and I overeat and she's pushing me too much and too hard to "change my ways."* _____ _____ _____
E	**E**xpress how you feel. Start your statements with "I." Remember that what you're talking about is how you feel and what you think. People can take "You" statements as accusations, which makes it more likely that there will be conflict in the conversation. *Example: I want to get better and will take steps to improve, but I need to do it at my own pace. I get even more stressed and depressed when I feel pressured.*

Your turn:

_____

_____

_____

Assert yourself.

Convey what you want to happen without being confrontational. You don't want a fight. You want to be clearly and effectively heard.

Example: I want and appreciate your help, but I will address my sleep and eating problems my way and at my own pace.

Your turn:

_____

_____

_____

Reinforce your request.

Make it clear to the other person how crucial your request is. Also, immediately express gratitude if they give in to what you want.

Example: I know my changes may not be as drastic and the results not as fast as you want, but I would really appreciate doing this my way. I would appreciate your support.

Your turn:

_____

_____

_____

Mindfulness.

Be mindful of YOUR wants and needs. Stay on track and maintain your position whatever the other person says. When other people don't agree with you, they may object, insist, dismiss, or argue with you. Whatever they do, don't be persuaded and stay true to what you want.

M

Example: I hear you. But that's not what will work best for me, and what's best for me and my depression is to make the positive changes I want on my terms.

Your turn:

_____

_____

_____

Appear confident.

Don't hesitate and give the other party a chance to argue. Show confidence through verbal and non-verbal cues, but don't be intimidating. Don't raise your voice or stare the other person down. Remember to be consistent too. For example, don't maintain eye contact and immediately look away after making your request.

A

How do you want to show confidence?

Example: Sit or stand tall, roll your shoulders back, and maintain eye contact. Next, say, "I hope you understand because I'm not going to change my mind on this."

_____

_____

_____

_____

Negotiate.

If the other person(s) won't give in, it's time to negotiate. This will give you both time to devise a solution that will work. You can suggest a way to move forward or ask the other person what they think should happen next.

Example: How about I make an exercise routine and schedule. It may not be as rigorous as you suggest, but it will still be progress. We can both monitor how things are in a week or so. What do you think?

Your turn:

_____

_____

_____

Worksheet: GIVE

GIVE is about relationship effectiveness. This exercise is about maintaining relationships with others by fostering positive interactions. Basically, you want the other person to feel good in the conversation so that they're more likely to grant your request.

G	Be **G**entle. Don't demand, be disrespectful or be abrasive when making a request. Also, don't say or do anything that could make the other person feel bad. Simply put—be nice! List five ways to ask for something in a nice way. *Examples: "Is it okay if we..." or "Do you mind if..."* 1. _____ 2. _____ 3. _____ 4. _____ 5. _____
I	Act **I**nterested. Relationships are not all about you. Communicating is about wanting to be heard and hearing what the other person says. As such, pay attention to the person(s) with whom you're conversing. (See also Active Listening, page 136.) List five ways you convey interest. *Example: look at the other person and maintain eye contact, don't interrupt, respond to what was said, etc.*

1. _____

2. _____

3. _____

4. _____

5. _____

Validate.

Show that you understand what the other person is thinking and feeling. (See also Active Listening, page 136.)

List five ways you validate others.

Examples: Say, "If I understand you correctly, you mean..." or "Oh wow, I never knew that's what it meant for you."

1. _____ .

2. _____

3. _____

4. _____

5. _____

Show an Easy Manner.

Act in a friendly manner. Be casual so the other person thinks you're asking, not telling them what to do. People will feel more at ease and be more open to what you want if you have a friendly attitude.

List 5 ways you can show friendliness.

Examples: smile, adopt a relaxed posture, make eye contact, etc.

1. _____

2. _____

3. _____

4. _____

5. _____

Worksheet: FAST

FAST is about self-respect effectiveness. It's about protecting yourself from betraying your values and beliefs to receive approval or get what you want.

F	## Be Fair. Be fair to yourself and other people during conversations. As you make your request, ensure it isn't anything beyond the other person's abilities to grant. Also, ensure that you ask politely. Don't make demands or make the other person feel threatened or guilty if they don't grant your request. Practice making a request fairly and reasonably. *Example: I'd like to take Friday off, please. I have an appointment with my therapist.* Your turn: _____ _____ _____
A	## No Apologies. Don't apologize or over-apologize. There's no need to apologize for making a request, and you shouldn't say sorry if you want to say "No" to someone. Practice making a request without apologizing: *Example: I'd like to take Friday off, please. I have an appointment with my therapist.* *NOT: I'm so sorry to ask, but can I please take Friday off? I have an appointment with my therapist. I'm really sorry about not asking earlier.*

Your turn:

_____

_____

_____

Practice saying "No" to someone without apologizing:

Example: I don't want to go out drinking this weekend.

NOT: I feel bad about this, but I'm sorry, I don't want to go out drinking this weekend. Sorry!

Your turn:

_____

_____

_____

Stick to your <u>V</u>alues.

Don't betray your values just because the other person doesn't like your request or does not agree with you. And don't betray your values if someone is nagging you to say "Yes" to something.

Practice sticking to your values when making a request:

Example: I need Friday off for my mental health. That's most important to me.

Your turn:

_____

_____

_____

Practice sticking to your values and saying "No" no matter what the other person says, does, or tries to get you to do.

Example: I understand you need more hands at work, but I need Friday off for my mental health. That's most important to me.

Your turn:

_____

_____

_____

Be Truthful.

Don't lie, dramatize or exaggerate to get what you want or to get out of something you don't want to do. Honesty is the best policy.

Practice honesty when making a request:
Example: I've been struggling and need a mental day off to take care of myself.

Your turn:

_____

_____

_____

Practice honesty when saying "No:
Example: I don't want to go out drinking this weekend.
NOT: Oh, THIS weekend? Oh man, I want to, but I can't. It's, uh... my mom's birthday! The family would hate my guts if I didn't show up.

Your turn:

_____

_____

_____

Chapter Highlights:

- **Dialectical Behavior Therapy** (DBT) is a type of therapy that combines cognitive-behavioral techniques (CBT) with mindfulness practices.
- Research shows that DBT is **highly effective in treating depression**.
- **Dialectics** is a way of thinking and solving problems that involve recognizing and balancing different ideas or points of view.
- **DBT Core Concepts**: Acceptance and Change.
- **DBT Core Skills**: Mindfulness, Distress Tolerance, Emotion Regulation and Interpersonal Effectiveness. Related worksheets for each skill featuring depression-specific situations are provided.

Continuing the Road to Happiness

Healing is a choice. It's not an easy one because it takes work to turn around and face the pain. But in the end, it's worth it."
— *Marianne Williamson*

Self-Esteem: The Link Between Self-Perception and Depression

Low self-esteem and depression are intimately linked, and those with poor self-esteem are at a higher risk of developing depression.[59,60]

People with poor self-esteem have a negative perception of themselves and their talents. They may feel inadequate, useless, or irrelevant. These negative ideas about yourself can make it hard to deal with stressful situations and make you feel like you have no control or hope, leading to depression.

As such, addressing poor self-esteem can be an essential component of depression treatment. Here are some suggestions for increasing self-esteem:

1. **Practice self-care.** Self-care is caring for your physical, emotional, and mental well-being. It involves deciding to prioritize your own health and happiness and taking steps to meet your own needs. Self-care aims to promote a sense of balance, reduce stress, and help you feel your best. By taking care of yourself, you can better manage the challenges and demands of everyday life.

List at least five (5) self-care activities you're doing right now.

Examples: mental breaks, short walks in nature, drinking enough water, etc.

1. _____
2. _____
3. _____
4. _____
5. _____

List at least five (5) self-care activities you plan to do from now on.

Examples: getting enough sleep, eating healthy foods, exercising, making time for hobbies, etc.

1. _____
2. _____
3. _____
4. _____
5. _____

2. **Challenge negative self-talk.** Recognize your inner critic and confront negative beliefs by challenging their authenticity and replacing them with more positive and realistic ones. Here are some suggestions for doing this:

a.) Identify the negative thought causing you distress or making you depressed. Please write it down or say it out loud.

Example: I'm such a lazy person. I can't even find the energy to get out of bed and brush my teeth.

Your turn:

_____
_____
_____

b.) Challenge your negative thought. What's the evidence supporting this thought? What evidence contradicts it? Practice dialectics and try to view the situation from a different perspective.

Example: I'm NOT a lazy person. My depression is the cause of my low energy, not me.

Your turn:

_____

_____

_____

c.) Once you've questioned the negative thought, replace it with a more positive and realistic one.

Example: I may often feel exhausted, but I still accomplish things. Last week, I spent quality time with my mom, and this week, I submitted an important work report a day ahead.

Your turn:

_____

_____

_____

d.) Practice self-compassion. Show kindness to yourself, just as you would a friend going through a difficult time. Remind yourself that it's okay to make mistakes and that you're doing the best you can.

e.) Challenging negative self-talk constantly. Repeat this exercise regularly to help train your brain to think more positively and realistically.

3. **Focus on your strengths.** Recognize your strengths, special skills, and successes. This will make you feel more capable and confident.

Despite my mental health problems, I did well in school and had good grades. Drawing was one of my special skills. While I was in Grade 6, I won an art award that I was especially proud of when I graduated elementary school. Later, I managed to get into an animation program for college in Ottawa. This was years *before* I saw a psychologist and was prescribed anti-anxiety meds, so I'm very proud of achieving this. I make it a point to remember this whenever I feel depressed.

Your turn:

_____

_____

_____

4. **Set achievable and realistic goals.** Set goals that are both attainable and practical. Divide them into smaller segments and celebrate your accomplishments along the way. By the way, a "goal" doesn't necessarily have to be big. For example, for someone suffering from depression, just "showing up" is already a major accomplishment, and you should be proud of that.

What's a goal you want to achieve?
Example: I want to sleep better to have more energy during the day.

Your turn:

_____

_____

_____

List the steps you should take to accomplish this goal.

Example: establish a sleep schedule, stop mindless phone scrolling in bed, de-clutter my bedroom, etc.

Your turn:

_____

_____

_____

5. **Surround yourself with positive people.** Spend time with people who make you feel good about yourself and who encourage and support you. According to studies, we are the average of the five individuals we spend the most time with.[61]. So be around optimistic people; their positivity will rub off on you!

    However, if you are surrounded by negative people who you cannot simply avoid (e.g., family members, friends, colleagues, etc.), make it a goal to spend less time with them. For example, skip the weekly Sunday dinners and attend every other week or once a month.

6. **Do things you like.** Participate in activities that you enjoy and make you feel good about yourself. This can range from reading a book to participating in a sport. (See also Build Positive Experiences, page 122.)

7. **Know that it's okay to prioritize YOU.** Self-care is not selfishness. When you care for yourself, you can better show up for others, including your family, friends, and colleagues. You're also more patient, compassionate, and empathetic when feeling rested, nourished, and emotionally balanced.

    On an airplane, the cabin attendant always tells passengers during the pre-flight briefing to "put your oxygen mask on first before assisting others." This

is before helping others. Why is this a key rule for staying alive? The reason is if you don't take care of yourself first, you won't be able to help other people with theirs. In other words, taking care of yourself allows you to show up as your best self, ultimately benefiting you and those you.

Building your self-esteem requires time and effort. Remember to be kind to yourself and concentrate on making tiny adjustments over time. Believe that you will get there, and you will!

Nutrition: Eat to Beat Depression

Nutritional psychiatry is a field of study that examines the link between what we eat and mental health. It's based on the idea that food affects our brain chemistry and can influence our mood, behavior, and cognitive function. It aims to use this knowledge to develop dietary interventions to improve mental health outcomes. This may involve promoting certain foods or nutrients or avoiding others, as well as incorporating dietary changes alongside other mental health treatments.

Nutritional psychiatry is a vast subject beyond this book's scope. So, we'll only cover a few basics here that are related to depression.

Here are some of the reasons why nutrition may be effective in depression:

1. **Nutrients influence brain function.** The brain requires nutrients such as vitamins, minerals, and vital fatty acids to function effectively. A diet deficient in these nutrients might cause brain chemistry alterations, contributing to depression.

   Example: Fruits and vegetables include essential vitamins and minerals that help with brain function and mood. Every day, try to consume various bright fruits and vegetables such as tomatoes, carrots, bell peppers, etc. As a general rule of thumb, the more color on your plate, the better.

2. **Blood sugar control.** A diet strong in refined carbs and sugar can cause blood sugar levels to soar and then plummet, resulting in weariness and mood swings. In contrast, a diet high in whole foods and complex carbs can help control blood sugar levels and provide a more consistent energy source.

Example: Healthy grains, such as brown rice, quinoa, and whole wheat bread, are high in fiber and B vitamins, which can help manage mood and blood sugar levels.

3. **Inflammation** has been related to depression, and some foods can raise inflammation while others can decrease it. Anti-inflammatory foods like fruits, vegetables, and healthy fats can help reduce inflammation and enhance mood.

   Example: Omega-3 fatty acids in fatty fish, walnuts, and flaxseeds have been demonstrated to reduce inflammation.

4. **Gut health**. The gut is considered by many as the "second brain" because it contains various neurotransmitters that influence mood and behavior. A high-fiber, fermented-food diet can help develop healthy gut flora, boosting mood.

   Example: Broccoli, peas, Brussels sprouts, and black beans are high-fiber foods. Kimchi, yogurt, and sauerkraut are examples of fermented foods.

Also, staying well-hydrated throughout the day is important. The recommended water intake for adults can vary depending on gender, body weight, physical activity level, and climate. However, a general guideline recommended by the Institute of Medicine (IOM) is that men should aim for about 3.7 liters (or about 13 cups) of total water intake per day. Women should aim for about 2.7 liters (or about 9 cups) of daily water intake.

Important: Before making any dietary changes, please consult with your doctor or healthcare provider.

Conclusion

"Healing comes from taking responsibility: to realize that it is you - and no one else - that creates your thoughts, your feelings, and your actions." — Peter Shepherd

---

People who suffer from depression don't feel happiness or at least find it very difficult to experience it. So, no, we cannot just "snap out of it" and "just be happy." During depressive episodes, we don't even have hope, so it's very hard to imagine being happy even though it's what we desire the most.

All I could think about for years was how to survive the day. So, I never really thought about how to make things better.

My mental health journey taught me that life doesn't just happen. As difficult as it may seem to believe, we have a lot of influence and power over how our lives turn out.

DBT is one of the tools I used to turn things around and be in control of my life instead of letting my OCD, GAD, and depression run my life. I sincerely hope you find it as helpful and effective as I have.

Here's a quick recap of what we covered in this book:

- Depression, or major depressive disorder (MDD): what it is, causes and symptoms, and currently known treatments.
- Living with Depression: Understand how MDD affects the brain and the body and how it influences relationships. Research shows that depression may be more prevalent in women. The section Depression in Women expounds on possible reasons for this.

- Dialectic Behavior Therapy (DBT) and its core concepts fundamentals (Acceptance and Change) and its primary skills (Mindfulness, Distress Tolerance, Emotion Regulation, and Interpersonal Effectiveness). Each concept and skill is explained in detail, and numerous exercises are provided to help you apply these skills daily.
- Additional tips: how to build your self-esteem and how to use nutrition to help treat depression.

"Believe in yourself and all that you are. Know that there is something inside you that is greater than any obstacle."
— Christian D. Larson

Appendix A – PHQ-9 Depression Self-Assessment

The following is the **Patient Health Questionnaire-9** (PHQ-9). It's a 9-point questionnaire that psychiatrist Dr. Robert L. Spitzer and his colleagues developed.[62] The purpose of PHQ-9 is to help assess the severity of depressive symptoms. It's considered a reliable and valid measure of depression severity.

Important: Please note that the PHQ-9 is meant to help you determine if your feelings, thoughts, or behaviors are signs of depression. It is NOT meant to be a diagnosis or a replacement for a professional evaluation. After you fill out this questionnaire and figure out how to score it, please share the results with your doctor or mental health professional.

Please answer the questions below to the best of your ability.

How often have you felt the following problems in the last two weeks? (Select your answer from the list on the right and circle it.)

	Not at all	Several days	More than half the days	Nearly every day
How often have you experienced a lack of interest or pleasure in doing things, especially activities you used to enjoy?	0	1	2	3
How often have you felt sad, down, or like there was no hope?	0	1	2	3
How often have you had sleep problems? (This can be trouble falling, staying, or sleeping too long.)	0	1	2	3
How often have you felt tired or like you didn't have much energy?	0	1	2	3
How often have you had eating issues like overeating or undereating?	0	1	2	3
How often have you had negative feelings about yourself? For example, have you often felt that you're always doing things "wrong" or often blame yourself for letting other people down?	0	1	2	3
How often have you had problems concentrating? For example, have you been having trouble focusing while reading the newspaper, watching a program, or when someone is speaking?	0	1	2	3
How often have you had problems moving or speaking? For example, have you been reacting slower that other people notice this change? Or perhaps, you're experiencing the opposite, such as being more fidgety or restless than usual?	0	1	2	3
How often have you thought about hurting yourself or dying?	0	1	2	3
Add total per column:				
Overall total:				

If you've encountered any of the symptoms listed above, how difficult has it been for you to function at work, at home, or get along with other people?

☐ Not difficult at all
☐ Somewhat difficult
☐ Very difficult
☐ Extremely difficult

Scoring:

1-9 = Low depression severity scale

Your score is low, indicating you may not suffer from depression. If you feel this is inaccurate, please learn and explore further or see a medical or mental health expert.

10-14 = Moderate depression severity range

Your score is in the moderate range, indicating that you may suffer from mild depression. As such, please seek professional advice from a medical or mental health expert as soon as possible.

15-27 = Severe depression severity range

Your score is in the high range, indicating that you may suffer from major depression. Please seek professional advice from a medical or mental health expert as soon as possible.

Appendix B – Journaling for Depression Relief

Journaling is a fantastic way to manage depression. It's a very personal activity, so there's no right or wrong way to do it. The goal is to use writing to connect with your feelings and learn more about yourself, helping you cope and heal from depression. Following are some guidelines.

1. **SET A SCHEDULE.**

   Set a journaling schedule. Find a place to sit down and write that is quiet and comfortable. Aim to set aside 15 to 20 minutes daily for your writing.

   What's the best time for you to journal?
   Example: In the morning, just after I wake up and before I go to work.

   _____

   _____

   _____

2. **USE PROMPTS.**

   Sometimes questions or prompts help start your journaling. For example, "*What's making me sad today?*" or "*What's making me happy today?*" or "*Did something trigger my feelings today?*" can help you get started and get your thoughts in order.

3. **NON-JUDGEMENTALLY.**

   Let yourself write freely and without judging what you write. Don't worry about spelling or grammar. Just write what you want to say.

4. **BE HONEST.**

   Tell the truth about how you feel. Write down any thoughts or feelings that are making you feel bad. It's important to recognize these feelings so you can get past them.

5. **GRATITUDE.**

Take a moment to think about the things you're thankful for. Every day, write down at least three things you're grateful for. This can assist you in shifting your focus from negative to positive aspects of your life. (See also Attitude of Gratitude, page **Error! Bookmark not defined.**.)

What are the three things you're grateful for today?
Example: unexpected call from my brother, eating my favorite salad for lunch, snuggling with my partner, etc.

_____

_____

_____

6. **SMALL GOALS.**

Write down one or two small goals you want to achieve each day. Setting small goals can help you feel like you're progressing and gaining speed.

What's your small goal today?
Example: wake up earlier, take short walks after lunch, etc.

_____

_____

_____

7. **REFLECT.**

Take a minute to think about what you've written. Ask yourself, "*What do I know now that I didn't know before?*" When you think about your thoughts and emotions, you can learn more about yourself and your feelings.

What have you discovered today?

Example: I discovered that if I MAKE TIME, I can go for short walks after lunch. I used to think I never had the time for it. I realize now that I was just making excuses.

Review Request

If you enjoyed this book or found it useful...

I'd like to ask you for a quick favor:

Please share your thoughts and leave a quick REVIEW. Your feedback matters and helps me make improvements to provide the best books possible.

Reviews are so helpful to both readers and authors, so any help would be greatly appreciated! You can leave a review here:

https://tinyurl.com/depression-review

Or by scanning the QR code below:

Also, please join my ARC team to get early access to my releases.

https://barretthuang.com/arc-team/

THANK YOU!

Further Reading

Be sure to check out my other bestselling DBT books in the Mental Health Therapy series. Here are some of the titles you can find:

- DBT Workbook for Adults
- DBT Workbook for Kids
- DBT Workbook for Teens
- The DBT Anger Management Workbook
- DBT Workbook for PTSD
- DBT Workbook for BPD

You can get them here:

https://tinyurl.com/mental-health-therapy

About the Author

Barrett Huang is an author and businessman. Barrett spent years discovering the best ways to manage his OCD, overcoming his anxiety, and learning to embrace life. Through his writing, he hopes to share his knowledge with readers, empowering people of all backgrounds with the tools and strategies they need to improve their mental wellbeing and be happy and healthy.

When not writing or running his business, Barrett loves to spend his time studying. He has majored in psychology and completed the DBT skills certificate course by Dr. Marsha Linehan. Barrett's idol is Bruce Lee, who said, "The key to immortality is first living a life worth remembering."

Learn more about Barrett's books here:

https://barretthuang.com/

Index

References

1 World Health Organization. (n.d.). *Depression*. World Health Organization. Retrieved March 1, 2023, from https://www.who.int/news-room/fact-sheets/detail/depression

2 U.S. Department of Health and Human Services. (n.d.). *Major depression*. National Institute of Mental Health. Retrieved March 1, 2023, from https://www.nimh.nih.gov/health/statistics/major-depression

3 Shadrina, M., Bondarenko, E. A., & Slominsky, P. A. (2018). Genetics factors in major depression disease. *Frontiers in Psychiatry*, 9. https://doi.org/10.3389/fpsyt.2018.00334

4 Levey, D. F., Stein, M. B., Wendt, F. R., Pathak, G. A., Zhou, H., Aslan, M., Quaden, R., Harrington, K. M., Nuñez, Y. Z., Overstreet, C., Radhakrishnan, K., Sanacora, G., McIntosh, A. M., Shi, J., Shringarpure, S. S., Concato, J., Polimanti, R., & Gelernter, J. (2021). Bi-ancestral depression GWAS in the million veteran program and meta-analysis in >1.2 million individuals highlight new therapeutic directions. *Nature Neuroscience*, 24(7), 954–963. https://doi.org/10.1038/s41593-021-00860-2

5 Brody, D. J., Pratt, L. A., & Hughes, J. (2018, February 13). *Prevalence of depression among adults aged 20 and over: United States, 2013–2016*. Centers for Disease Control and Prevention. Retrieved March 1, 2023, from https://www.cdc.gov/nchs/products/databriefs/db303.htm

6 Ng, C. W., How, C. H., & Ng, Y. P. (2017). Depression in primary care: Assessing suicide risk. *Singapore Medical Journal*, 58(2), 72–77. https://doi.org/10.11622/smedj.2017006

7 American Psychiatric Association. (2017). *Diagnostic And Statistical Manual Of Mental Disorders: DSM-5*.

8 France, C. M., Lysaker, P. H., & Robinson, R. P. (2007). The "chemical imbalance" explanation for depression: Origins, lay endorsement, and clinical implications. *Professional Psychology: Research and Practice*, 38(4), 411–420. https://doi.org/10.1037/0735-7028.38.4.411

9 Moncrieff, J., Cooper, R. E., Stockmann, T., Amendola, S., Hengartner, M. P., & Horowitz, M. A. (2022). The serotonin theory of depression: A Systematic Umbrella Review of the evidence. *Molecular Psychiatry*. https://doi.org/10.1038/s41380-022-01661-0

10 Lewis, G., Marston, L., Duffy, L., Freemantle, N., Gilbody, S., Hunter, R., Kendrick, T., Kessler, D., Mangin, D., King, M., Lanham, P., Moore, M., Nazareth, I., Wiles, N., Bacon, F., Bird, M., Brabyn, S., Burns, A., Clarke, C. S., ... Lewis, G. (2021). Maintenance or discontinuation of antidepressants in primary care. *New England Journal of Medicine*, *385*(14), 1257–1267. https://doi.org/10.1056/nejmoa2106356

11 Virk, G., Reeves, G., Rosenthal, N. E., Sher, L., & Postolache, T. T. (2009). Short exposure to light treatment improves depression scores in patients with seasonal affective disorder: A brief report. *International Journal on Disability and Human Development*, *8*(3). https://doi.org/10.1515/ijdhd.2009.8.3.283

12 Simon, G. (2005). Review: Bright light therapy and dawn simulation reduce symptom severity in seasonal affective disorder. *Evidence-Based Medicine*, *10*(5), 146–146. https://doi.org/10.1136/ebm.10.5.146

13 Craft, L. L., & Perna, F. M. (2004). The benefits of exercise for the clinically depressed. *The Primary Care Companion For CNS Disorders*, *6*(3). https://doi.org/10.4088/pcc.v06n0301

14 Schuch, F. B., & Stubbs, B. (2019). The role of exercise in preventing and treating depression. *Current Sports Medicine Reports*, *18*(8), 299–304. https://doi.org/10.1249/jsr.0000000000000620

15 Singh, B., Olds, T., Curtis, R., Dumuid, D., Virgara, R., Watson, A., Szeto, K., O'Connor, E., Ferguson, T., Eglitis, E., Miatke, A., Simpson, C. E. M., & Maher, C. (2023). Effectiveness of physical activity interventions for improving depression, anxiety and distress: An overview of systematic reviews. *British Journal of Sports Medicine*. https://doi.org/10.1136/bjsports-2022-106195

16 Saloheimo, H. P., Markowitz, J., Saloheimo, T. H., Laitinen, J. J., Sundell, J., Huttunen, M. O., A. Aro, T., Mikkonen, T. N., & O. Katila, H. (2016). Psychotherapy effectiveness for major depression: A randomized trial in a Finnish community. *BMC Psychiatry*, *16*(1). https://doi.org/10.1186/s12888-016-0838-1

17 Cuijpers, P., Quero, S., Noma, H., Ciharova, M., Miguel, C., Karyotaki, E., Cipriani, A., Cristea, I. A., & Furukawa, T. A. (2021). Psychotherapies for depression: A network meta-analysis covering efficacy, acceptability and long-term outcomes of all main treatment types. *World Psychiatry*, *20*(2), 283–293. https://doi.org/10.1002/wps.20860

18 Munder, T., Flückiger, C., Leichsenring, F., Abbass, A. A., Hilsenroth, M. J., Luyten, P., Rabung, S., Steinert, C., & Wampold, B. E. (2018). Is psychotherapy effective? A re-analysis of treatments for depression. *Epidemiology and Psychiatric Sciences*, *28*(03), 268–274. https://doi.org/10.1017/s2045796018000355

19 Qi, H., Ning, Y., Li, J., Guo, S., Chi, M., Gao, M., Guo, Y., Yang, Y., Peng, H., & Wu, K. (2014). Gray matter volume abnormalities in depressive patients with and without anxiety disorders. *Medicine*, *93*(29). https://doi.org/10.1097/md.0000000000000345

20 MediLexicon International. (n.d.). *Severe depression linked with inflammation in the brain*. Medical News Today. Retrieved March 1, 2023, from https://www.medicalnewstoday.com/articles/288715

21 Burtscher, J., Niedermeier, M., Hüfner, K., van den Burg, E., Kopp, M., Stoop, R., Burtscher, M., Gatterer, H., & Millet, G. P. (2022). The interplay of hypoxic and mental stress: Implications for anxiety and Depressive Disorders. *Neuroscience & Biobehavioral Reviews*, *138*, 104718. https://doi.org/10.1016/j.neubiorev.2022.104718

22 Lee, C.-H., & Giuliani, F. (2019). The role of inflammation in depression and fatigue. *Frontiers in Immunology*, *10*. https://doi.org/10.3389/fimmu.2019.01696

23 Cañas-González, B., Fernández-Nistal, A., Ramírez, J. M., & Martínez-Fernández, V. (2020). Influence of stress and depression on the immune system in patients evaluated in an anti-aging unit. *Frontiers in Psychology*, *11*. https://doi.org/10.3389/fpsyg.2020.01844

24 Whisman, M. A. (2001). The association between depression and marital dissatisfaction. *Marital and Family Processes in Depression: A Scientific Foundation for Clinical Practice.*, 3–24. https://doi.org/10.1037/10350-001

25 Salk, R. H., Hyde, J. S., & Abramson, L. Y. (2017). Gender differences in depression in representative national samples: Meta-analyses of diagnoses and symptoms. *Psychological Bulletin*, *143*(8), 783–822. https://doi.org/10.1037/bul0000102

26 Greenwood, S. (2023, March 1). *The enduring grip of the gender pay gap*. Pew Research Center's Social & Demographic Trends Project. Retrieved March 1, 2023, from https://www.pewresearch.org/social-trends/2023/03/01/the-enduring-grip-of-the-gender-pay-gap/

27 Montúfar, V. (2018, December 10). *Women are most likely to be affected by violence in the workplace, but we are all victims*. PSI. Retrieved March 1, 2023, from https://www.world-psi.org/en/women-are-most-likely-be-affected-violence-workplace-we-are-all-victims

28 Johnson, D. P., & Whisman, M. A. (2013). Gender differences in rumination: A meta-analysis. *Personality and Individual Differences, 55*(4), 367–374. https://doi.org/10.1016/j.paid.2013.03.019

29 Nolen-Hoeksema, S. (2000). The role of rumination in depressive disorders and mixed anxiety/depressive symptoms. *Journal of Abnormal Psychology, 109*(3), 504–511. https://doi.org/10.1037/0021-843x.109.3.504

30 Treynor, W., Gonzalez, R., & Nolen-Hoeksema, S. (2003). Rumination Reconsidered: A Psychometric Analysis. *Cognitive Therapy and Research, 27*(3), 247–259. https://doi.org/10.1023/a:1023910315561

31 Pederson, L., & Pederson, C. S. (2017). Module 1: Dialectics. In *The Expanded Dialectical Behavior Therapy Skills Training Manual: DBT for Self-Help, and Individual and Group Treatment Settings* (pp. 41–42). PESI Publishing & Media.

32 Lynch, T. R., Morse, J. Q., Mendelson, T., & Robins, C. J. (2003). Dialectical behavior therapy for depressed older adults: a randomized pilot study. *The American Journal of Geriatric Psychiatry: Official Journal of the American Association for Geriatric Psychiatry, 11*(1), 33–45.

33 Feldman, G., Harley, R., Kerrigan, M., Jacobo, M., & Fava, M. (2009). Change in emotional processing during a dialectical behavior therapy-based Skills Group for major depressive disorder. *Behaviour Research and Therapy, 47*(4), 316–321. https://doi.org/10.1016/j.brat.2009.01.005

34 Saito, E., Tebbett-Mock, A. A., & McGee, M. (2020). Dialectical behavior therapy decreases depressive symptoms among adolescents in an acute-care inpatient unit. *Journal of Child and Adolescent Psychopharmacology, 30*(4), 244–249. https://doi.org/10.1089/cap.2019.0149

35 Zaccaro, A., Piarulli, A., Laurino, M., Garbella, E., Menicucci, D., Neri, B., & Gemignani, A. (2018). How breath-control can change your life: A systematic review on psycho-physiological correlates of slow breathing. *Frontiers in Human Neuroscience, 12*. https://doi.org/10.3389/fnhum.2018.00353

36 Valenza, M. C., Valenza-Peña, G., Torres-Sánchez, I., González-Jiménez, E., Conde-Valero, A., & Valenza-Demet, G. (2013). Effectiveness of controlled

breathing techniques on anxiety and depression in hospitalized patients with COPD: A randomized clinical trial. *Respiratory Care, 59*(2), 209–215. https://doi.org/10.4187/respcare.02565

37 Kyriakoulis, P., Kyrios, M., Nardi, A. E., Freire, R. C., & Schier, M. (2021). The implications of the diving response in reducing panic symptoms. *Frontiers in Psychiatry, 12.* https://doi.org/10.3389/fpsyt.2021.784884

38 Ito, E., Shima, R., & Yoshioka, T. (2019). A novel role of oxytocin: Oxytocin-induced well-being in humans. *Biophysics and Physicobiology, 16,* 132–139. https://doi.org/10.2142/biophysico.16.0_132

39 *Serotonin: What is it, Function & Levels.* Cleveland Clinic. (n.d.). Retrieved March 1, 2023, from https://my.clevelandclinic.org/health/articles/22572-serotonin

40 Weir, K. (2011, December). *The exercise effect.* Monitor on Psychology. Retrieved February 1, 2023, from https://www.apa.org/monitor/2011/12/exercise

41 Puetz, T. W. (2006). Physical activity and feelings of energy and fatigue. *Sports Medicine, 36*(9), 767–780. https://doi.org/10.2165/00007256-200636090-00004

42 Dossey, L. (2018). The Helper's High. *EXPLORE, 14*(6), 393–399. https://doi.org/10.1016/j.explore.2018.10.003

43 Ellison, C. G., Bradshaw, M., Flannelly, K. J., & Galek, K. C. (2014). Prayer, attachment to god, and symptoms of anxiety-related disorders among U.S. adults. *Sociology of Religion, 75*(2), 208–233. https://doi.org/10.1093/socrel/srt079

44 Author, P. C. G. (2014, September 18). *Prayer and mental health: What does research say?* Psych Central. Retrieved April 1, 2023, from https://psychcentral.com/blog/new-study-examines-the-effects-of-prayer-on-mental-health

45 Pally, R., & Olds, D. (2018). Emotional processing: The mind-body connection. *The Mind-Brain Relationship,* 73–104. https://doi.org/10.4324/9780429482465-4

46 Seward, E. A., & Kelly, S. (2016). Dietary nitrogen alters codon bias and genome composition in parasitic microorganisms. *Genome Biology, 17*(1). https://doi.org/10.1186/s13059-016-1087-9

47 Lane, M. M., Gamage, E., Travica, N., Dissanayaka, T., Ashtree, D. N., Gauci, S., Lotfaliany, M., O'Neil, A., Jacka, F. N., & Marx, W. (2022). Ultra-processed food consumption and mental health: A systematic review and meta-analysis of observational studies. *Nutrients*, *14*(13), 2568. https://doi.org/10.3390/nu14132568

48 Firth, J., Gangwisch, J. E., Borsini, A., Wootton, R. E., & Mayer, E. A. (2020). Food and mood: How do diet and nutrition affect mental wellbeing? *BMJ*, m2382. https://doi.org/10.1136/bmj.m2382

49 Keyes, K. M., Allel, K., Staudinger, U. M., Ornstein, K. A., & Calvo, E. (2019). Alcohol consumption predicts incidence of depressive episodes across 10 years among older adults in 19 countries. *International Review of Neurobiology*, 1–38. https://doi.org/10.1016/bs.irn.2019.09.001

50 Chattu, V. K., Aeri, B. T., & Khanna, P. (2019). Nutritional aspects of depression in adolescents - A systematic review. *International Journal of Preventive Medicine*, *10*(1), 42. https://doi.org/10.4103/ijpvm.ijpvm_400_18

51 Nawrot, P., Jordan, S., Eastwood, J., Rotstein, J., Hugenholtz, A., & Feeley, M. (2003). Effects of caffeine on human health. *Food Additives and Contaminants*, *20*(1), 1–30. https://doi.org/10.1080/0265203021000007840

52 Higdon, J. V., & Frei, B. (2006). Coffee and health: A review of recent human research. *Critical Reviews in Food Science and Nutrition*, *46*(2), 101–123. https://doi.org/10.1080/10408390500400009

53 Watson, N. F., Badr, M. S., Belenky, G., Bliwise, D. L., Buxton, O. M., Buysse, D., Dinges, D. F., Gangwisch, J., Grandner, M. A., Kushida, C., Malhotra, R. K., Martin, J. L., Patel, S. R., Quan, S., & Tasali, E. (2015). Recommended amount of sleep for a healthy adult: A joint consensus statement of the American Academy of Sleep Medicine and Sleep Research Society. *SLEEP*. https://doi.org/10.5665/sleep.4716

54 Wang, K., Yang, Y., Zhang, T., Ouyang, Y., Liu, B., & Luo, J. (2020). The relationship between physical activity and emotional intelligence in college students: The mediating role of self-efficacy. *Frontiers in Psychology*, *11*. https://doi.org/10.3389/fpsyg.2020.00967

55 Li, J., Huang, Z., Si, W., & Shao, T. (2022). The effects of physical activity on positive emotions in children and adolescents: A systematic review and meta-analysis. *International Journal of Environmental Research and Public Health*, *19*(21), 14185. https://doi.org/10.3390/ijerph192114185

56 Segrin, C. (1996). Interpersonal communication problems associated with depression and loneliness. *Handbook of Communication and Emotion*, 215–242. https://doi.org/10.1016/b978-012057770-5/50010-2

57 Chandrasekaran, B., Van Engen, K., Xie, Z., Beevers, C. G., & Maddox, W. T. (2014). Influence of depressive symptoms on speech perception in adverse listening conditions. *Cognition and Emotion*, *29*(5), 900–909. https://doi.org/10.1080/02699931.2014.944106

58 Martínez, R., Senra, C., Fernández-Rey, J., & Merino, H. (2020). Sociotropy, autonomy and emotional symptoms in patients with major depression or generalized anxiety: The mediating role of rumination and immature defenses. *International Journal of Environmental Research and Public Health*, *17*(16), 5716. https://doi.org/10.3390/ijerph17165716

59 Orth, U., & Robins, R. W. (2013). Understanding the link between low self-esteem and depression. *Current Directions in Psychological Science*, *22*(6), 455–460. https://doi.org/10.1177/0963721413492763

60 Lee, J. Y., Patel, M., & Scior, K. (2023). Self-esteem and its relationship with depression and anxiety in adults with intellectual disabilities: A systematic literature review. *Journal of Intellectual Disability Research*. https://doi.org/10.1111/jir.13025

61 Groth, A. (2012, July 24). *You're the average of the five people you spend the most time with*. Business Insider. Retrieved April 21, 2022, from https://www.businessinsider.com/jim-rohn-youre-the-average-of-the-five-people-you-spend-the-most-time-with-2012-7

62 Kroenke, K., Spitzer, R. L., & Williams, J. B. (2001). The PHQ-9. *Journal of General Internal Medicine*, *16*(9), 606–613. https://doi.org/10.1046/j.1525-1497.2001.016009606.x

Made in United States
Orlando, FL
31 March 2024

4531 1440R00096